The Country Wife by William Wycherley

A comedy, Acted at the Theatre Royal and first performed on January 12th, 1675.

William Wycherley was born at Clive near Shrewsbury, Shropshire and baptised on April 8th, 1641 at Whitchurch in Hampshire where it is thought he spent some time before his family settled in Malappuram, India.

At the age of he was sent to France to be educated in France. It was here that he converted to Roman Catholicism. Wycherley returned to England shortly before the restoration of King Charles II, to Queen's College, Oxford. Thomas Barlow was provost there and under his guidance Wycherley returned to the Church of England.

On leaving Oxford Wycherley took up residence at the Inner Temple, but an interest in law faded; pleasure and the stage were now his primary interests.

His play, Love in a Wood, was produced early in 1671 at the Theatre Royal, Drury Lane. It was daring and he became the talk of the Court. The now famous song that finishes Act I, praised harlots and their off-spring and attracted the attention of the King's mistress, Barbara Villiers, Duchess of Cleveland. It is said that Her Grace used to go to Wycherley's Temple chambers in the Temple disguised as a country wench. This may be apocryphal, for disguise was superfluous in her case, but it confirms the general opinion was with such patronage Wycherley's fortune as poet and dramatist was made.

Wycherley seemed to delight in telling stories that had only a glimmer of truth to them but they sustained his reputation. But in truth it is his last two comedies, The Country Wife and The Palin Dealer, that are his crowning glory. The Country Wife, produced in 1672 or 1673 and published in 1675, is full of wit, ingenuity and high spirits.

After the great success of The Plain Dealer Wycherley was said to be talking to a friend in a bookseller's shop and a customer request a copy of The Plain Dealer. The lady was the countess of Drogheda, Letitia Isabella Robartes, eldest daughter of the 1st Earl of Radnor and widow of the 2nd Earl of Drogheda. An introduction was secured and soon marriage. Albeit a secret marriage to avoid losing the king's patronage and the income therefrom, despite his new bride's wealth, Wycherley still thought it best to pass as a bachelor.

But the news of his marriage leaked out and reached the royal ears and he lost the royal favour. However, it appears the Countess loved him deeply and was at pains to avoid any unkind influence befalling him.

Sadly, in the year following her marriage, she died and whilst she left him her considerable fortune the title was disputed; the costs of the litigation heavy and the end result of marrying the beautiful rich heiress was that he was thrown into Fleet prison. He remained there for seven years, being released only after James II had been so sated by seeing The Plain Dealer that he paid off Wycherley's execution creditor and settled on him a pension of £200 a year.

Other debts still troubled Wycherley, however, and he never was released from his embarrassments, not even after succeeding to a life estate in the family property.

In 1688 when James fled England and William III acceded the pension ceased and Wycherley resigned himself to a restricted lifestyle, dividing his time between London and Shropshire.

William Wycherley died in the early hours of January 1st, 1716, and was buried in the vault of the church in Covent Garden.

Index of Contents

DRAMATIS PERSONAE

Mr. Horner,	Mr. Hart.
Mr. Harcourt,	Mr. Kenaston.
Mr. Dorilant,	Mr. Lydal.
Mr. Pinchwife,	Mr. Mohun.
Mr. Sparkish,	Mr. Haynes.
Sir Jaspar Fidget,	Mr. Cartwright.
Mrs. Margery Pinchwife,	Mrs. Bowtel.
Mrs. Alithea,	Mrs. James.
My Lady Fidget,	Mrs. Knep.
Mrs. Dainty Fidget,	Mrs. Corbet.
Mrs. Squeamish.	Mrs. Wyatt.

Old Lady Squeamish.   Mrs. Rutter.
Waiters, Servants, and Attendants.
A Boy.
A Quack,   Mr. Schotterel.
Lucy, Alithea's Maid,   Mrs. Cory.

The SCENE—London

PROLOGUE, spoken by Mr. Hart

Poets like Cudgel'd Bullys, never do
At first, or second blow, submit to you;
But will provoke you still, and ne're have done,
Till you are weary first, with laying on:
The late so bafled Scribler of this day,
Though he stands trembling, bids me boldly say,
What we, before most Playes are us'd to do,
For Poets out of fear, first draw on you;
In a fierce Prologue, the still Pit defie,
And e're you speak, like Castril, give the lye;
But though our Bayses Batles oft I've fought,
And with bruis'd knuckles, their dear Conquests bought;
Nay, never yet fear'd Odds upon the Stage,
In Prologue dare not Hector with the Age,
But wou'd take Quarter from your saving hands,
Though Bayse within all yielding Countermands,
Says you Confed'rate Wits no Quarter give,
Ther'fore his Play shan't ask your leave to live:
Well, let the vain rash Fop, by huffing so,
Think to obtain the better terms of you;
But we the Actors humbly will submit,
Now, and at any time, to a full Pit;
Nay, often we anticipate your rage,
And murder Poets for you, on our Stage:
We set no Guards upon our Tyring-Room,
But when with flying Colours, there you come,
We patiently you see, give up to you,
Our Poets, Virgins, nay our Matrons too.

ACT I.

SCENE I

Enter **HORNER**, and **QUACK** following him at a distance.

HORNER
A quack is as fit for a Pimp, as a Midwife for a Bawd; they are still but in their way, both helpers of Nature.—[aside.]—Well, my dear Doctor, hast thou done what I desired.

QUACK
I have undone you for ever with the Women, and reported you throughout the whole Town as bad as an Eunuch, with as much trouble as if I had made you one in earnest.

HORNER
But have you told all the Midwives you know, the Orange Wenches at the Playhouses, the City Husbands, and old Fumbling Keepers of this end of the Town, for they'l be the readiest to report it.

QUACK
I have told all the Chamber-maids, Waiting women, Tyre women, and Old women of my acquaintance; nay, and whisper'd it as a secret to'em, and to the Whisperers of Whitehal; so that you need not doubt 'twill spread, and you will be as odious to the handsome young Women, as—

HORNER
As the small Pox.—Well—

QUACK
And to the married Women of this end of the Town, as—

HORNER
As the great ones; nay, as their own Husbands.

QUACK
And to the City Dames as Annis-seed Robin of filthy and contemptible memory; and they will frighten their Children with your name, especially their Females.

HORNER
And cry Horner's coming to carry you away: I am only afraid 'twill not be believ'd; you told'em 'twas by an English-French disaster, and an English-French Chirurgeon, who has given me at once, not only a Cure, but an Antidote for the future, against that damn'd malady, and that worse distemper, love, and all other Womens evils.

QUACK
Your late journey into France has made it the more credible, and your being here a fortnight before you appear'd in publick, looks as if you apprehended the shame, which I wonder you do not: Well I have been hired by young Gallants to bely'em t'other way; but you are the first wou'd be thought a Man unfit for Women.

HORNER
Dear Mr. Doctor, let vain Rogues be contented only to be thought abler Men than they are, generally 'tis all the pleasure they have, but mine lyes another way.

QUACK

You take, methinks, a very preposterous way to it, and as ridiculous as if we Operators in Physick, shou'd put forth Bills to disparage our Medicaments, with hopes to gain Customers.

HORNER

Doctor, there are Quacks in love, as well as Physick, who get but the fewer and worse Patients, for their boasting; a good name is seldom got by giving it ones self, and Women no more than honour are compass'd by bragging: Come, come Doctor, the wisest Lawyer never discovers the merits of his cause till the tryal; the wealthiest Man conceals his riches, and the cunning Gamster his play; Shy Husbands and Keepers like old Rooks are not to be cheated, but by a new unpractis'd trick; false friendship will pass now no more than false dice upon'em, no, not in the City.

[Enter **BOY**.

BOY

There are two Ladies and a Gentleman coming up.

HORNER

A Pox, some unbelieving Sisters of my former acquaintance, who I am afraid, expect their sense shou'd be satisfy'd of the falsity of the report.

[Enter **SIR JASPAR FIDGET, LADY FIDGET,** and **MRS DAINTY FIDGET**.

No—this formal Fool and Women!

QUACK

His Wife and Sister.

SIR JASPAR

My Coach breaking just now before your door Sir, I look upon as an occasional repremand to me Sir, for not kissing your hands Sir, since your coming out of France Sir; and so my disaster Sir, has been my good fortune Sir; and this is my Wife, and Sister Sir.

HORNER

What then, Sir?

SIR JASPAR

My Lady, and Sister, Sir.—Wife, this is Master Horner.

LADY FIDGET

Master Horner, Husband!

SIR JASPAR

My Lady, my Lady Fidget, Sir.

HORNER

So, Sir.

SIR JASPAR

Won't you be acquainted with her Sir? So the report is true, I find by his coldness or aversion to the Sex; but I'll play the wag with him. [Aside.] Pray salute my Wife, my Lady, Sir.

HORNER

I will kiss no Mans Wife, Sir, for him, Sir; I have taken my eternal leave, Sir, of the Sex already, Sir.

SIR JASPAR

Hah, hah, hah; I'll plague him yet.[aside.]
Not know my Wife, Sir?

HORNER

I do know your Wife, Sir, she's a Woman, Sir, and consequently a Monster, Sir, a greater Monster than a Husband, Sir.

SIR JASPAR

A Husband; how, Sir?

HORNER

So, Sir; but I make no more Cuckholds, Sir.

[Makes horns.

SIR JASPAR

Hah, hah, hah, Mercury, Mercury.

LADY FIDGET

Pray, Sir Jaspar, let us be gone from this rude fellow.

MRS DAINTY FIDGET

Who, by his breeding, wou'd think, he had ever been in France?

LADY FIDGET

Foh, he's but too much a French fellow, such as hate Women of quality and virtue, for their love to their Husband, Sr. Jaspar; a Woman is hated by'em as much for loving her Husband, as for loving their Money: But pray, let's be gone.

HORNER

You do well, Madam, for I have nothing that you came for: I have brought over not so much as a Bawdy Picture, new Postures, nor the second Part of the Escole de Fides; Nor—

QUACK

Hold for shame, Sir; what d'y mean? you'l ruine your self for ever with the Sex—.

[Apart to **HORNER**.

SIR JASPAR

Hah, hah, hah, he hates Women perfectly I find.

MRS DAINTY FIDGET
What pitty 'tis he shou'd.

LADY FIDGET
Ay, he's a base rude Fellow for't; but affectation makes not a Woman more odious to them, than Virtue.

HORNER
Because your Virtue is your greatest affectation, Madam.

LADY FIDGET
How, you sawcy Fellow, wou'd you wrong my honour?

HORNER
If I cou'd.

LADY FIDGET
How d'y mean, Sir?

SIR JASPAR
Hah, hah, hah, no he can't wrong your Ladyships honour, upon my honour; he poor Man—hark you in your ear—a meer Eunuch.

LADY FIDGET
O filthy French Beast, foh, foh; why do we stay? let's be gone; I can't endure the sight of him.

SIR JASPAR
Stay, but till the Chairs come, they'l be here presently.

LADY FIDGET
No, no.

SIR JASPAR
Nor can I stay longer; 'tis—let me see, a quarter and a half quarter of a minute past eleven; the Council will be sate, I must away: business must be preferr'd always before Love and Ceremony with the wise Mr. Horner.

HORNER
And the Impotent Sir Jaspar.

SIR JASPAR
Ay, ay, the impotent Master Horner, hah, ha, ha.

LADY FIDGET
What leave us with a filthy Man alone in his lodgings?

SIR JASPAR

He's an innocent Man now, you know; pray stay, I'll hasten the Chaires to you.—Mr. Horner your Servant, I shou'd be glad to see you at my house; pray, come and dine with me, and play at Cards with my Wife after dinner, you are fit for Women at that game; yet hah, ha—['Tis as much a Husbands prudence to provide innocent diversion for a Wife, as to hinder her unlawful pleasures; and he had better employ her, than let her employ her self. [Aside.
Farewel.

[Exit **SIR JASPAR**.

HORNER
Your Servant Sr. Jaspar.

LADY FIDGET
I will not stay with him, foh—

HORNER
Nay, Madam, I beseech you stay, if it be but to see, I can be as civil to Ladies yet, as they wou'd desire.

LADY FIDGET
No, no, foh, you cannot be civil to Ladies.

MRS DAINTY FIDGET
You as civil as Ladies wou'd desire.

LADY FIDGET
No, no, no, foh, foh, foh.

[Exeunt **LADY FIDGET** and **MRS DAINTY FIDGET**.

QUACK
Now I think, I, or you your self rather, have done your business with the Women.

HORNER
Thou art an Ass; don't you see already upon the report and my carriage, this grave Man of business leaves his Wife in my lodgings, invites me to his house and wife, who before wou'd not be acquainted with me out of jealousy.

QUACK
Nay; by this means you may be the more acquainted with the Husbands, but the less with the Wives.

HORNER
Let me alone, if I can but abuse the Husbands, I'll soon disabuse the Wives: Stay—I'll reckon you up the advantages, I am like to have by my Stratagem: First, I shall be rid of all my old Acquaintances, the most insatiable sorts of Duns, that invade our Lodgings in a morning: And next, to the pleasure of making a New Mistriss, is that of being rid of an old One, and of all old Debts; Love when it comes to be so, is paid the most unwillingly.

QUACK

Well, you may be so rid of your old Acquaintances; but how will you get any new Ones?

HORNER
Doctor, thou wilt never make a good Chymist, thou art so incredulous and impatient; ask but all the young Fellows of the Town, if they do not loose more time like Huntsmen, in starting the game, than in running it down; one knows not where to find'em. who will, or will not; Women of Quality are so civil, you can hardly distinguish love from good breeding, and a Man is often mistaken; but now I can be sure, she that shews an aversion to me loves the sport, as those Women that are gone, whom I warrant to be right: And then the next thing, is your Women of Honour, as you call'em, are only chary of their reputations, not their Persons, and 'tis scandal they wou'd avoid, not Men: Now may I have, by the reputation of an Eunuch, the Priviledges of One; and be seen in a Ladies Chamber, in a morning as early as her Husband; kiss Virgins before their Parents, or Lovers; and may be in short the Pas par tout of the Town. Now Doctor.

QUACK
Nay, now you shall be the Doctor; and your Process is so new, that we do not know but it may succeed.

HORNER
Not so new neither, Probatum est Doctor.

QUACK
Well, I wish you luck and many Patients whil'st I go to mine.

[Exit. **QUACK**

[Enter **HARCOURT**, and **DORILANT** to **HORNER**.

HARCOURT
Come, your appearance at the Play yesterday, has I hope hardned you for the future against the Womens contempt, and the Mens raillery; and now you'l abroad as you were wont.

HORNER
Did I not bear it bravely?

DORILANT
With a most Theatrical impudence; nay more than the Orange-wenches shew there, or a drunken vizard Mask, or a great belly'd Actress; nay, or the most impudent of Creatures, an ill Poet; or what is yet more impudent, a second-hand Critick.

HORNER
But what say the Ladies, have they no pitty?

HARCOURT
What Ladies? the vizard Masques you know never pitty a Man when all's gone, though in their Service.

DORILANT
And for the Women in the boxes, you'd never pitty them, when 'twas in your power.

HARCOURT

They say 'tis pitty, but all that deal with common Women shou'd be serv'd so.

DORILANT

Nay, I dare swear, they won't admit you to play at Cards with them, go to Plays with'em, or do the little duties which other Shadows of men, are wont to do for'em.

HORNER

Who do you call Shadows of Men?

DORILANT

Half Men.

HORNER

What Boyes?

DORILANT

Ay your old Boyes, old beaux Garcons, who like super-annuated Stallions are suffer'd to run, feed, and whinney with the Mares as long as they live, though they can do nothing else.

HORNER

Well a Pox on love and wenching, Women serve but to keep a Man from better Company; though I can't enjoy them, I shall you the more: good fellowship and friendship, are lasting, rational and manly pleasures.

HARCOURT

For all that give me some of those pleasures, you call effeminate too, they help to relish one another.

HORNER

They disturb one another.

HARCOURT

No, Mistresses are like Books; if you pore upon them too much, they doze you, and make you unfit for Company; but if us'd discreetly, you are the fitter for conversation by'em.

DORILANT

A Mistress shou'd be like a little Country retreat near the Town, not to dwell in constantly, but only for a night and away; to tast the Town the better when a Man returns.

HORNER

I tell you, 'tis as hard to be a good Fellow, a good Friend, and a Lover of Women, as 'tis to be a good Fellow, a good Friend, and a Lover of Money: You cannot follow both, then choose your side; Wine gives you liberty, Love takes it away.

DORILANT

Gad, he's in the right on't.

HORNER

Wine gives you joy, Love grief and tortures; besides the Chirurgeon's Wine makes us witty, Love only Sots: Wine makes us sleep, Love breaks it.

DORILANT
By the World he has reason, Harcourt.

HORNER
Wine makes—

DORILANT
Ay, Wine makes us—makes us Princes, Love makes us Beggars, poor Rogues, y gad—and Wine—

HORNER
So, there's one converted.—No, no, Love and Wine, Oil and Vinegar.

HARCOURT
I grant it; Love will still be uppermost.

HORNER
Come, for my part I will have only those glorious, manly pleasures of being very drunk, and very slovenly.

[Enter **BOY**.

BOY
Mr. Sparkish is below, Sir.

HARCOURT
What, my dear Friend! a Rogue that is fond of me, only I think for abusing him.

DORILANT
No, he can no more think the Men laugh at him, than that Women jilt him, his opinion of himself is so good.

HORNER
Well, there's another pleasure by drinking, I thought not of; I shall loose his acquaintance, because he cannot drink; and you know 'tis a very hard thing to be rid of him, for he's one of those nauseous offerers at wit, who like the worst Fidlers run themselves into all Companies.

HARCOURT
One, that by being in the Company of Men of sense wou'd pass for one.

HORNER
And may so to the short-sighed World, as a false Jewel amongst true ones, is not discern'd at a distance; his Company is as troublesome to us, as a Cuckolds, when you have a mind to his Wife's.

HARCOURT

No, the Rogue will not let us enjoy one another, but ravishes our conversation, though he signifies no more to't, than Sir Martin Mar-all's gaping, and auker'd thrumming upon the Lute, does to his Man's Voice, and Musick.

DORILANT

And to pass for a wit in Town, shewes himself a fool every night to us, that are guilty of the plot.

HORNER

Such wits as he, are, to a Company of reasonable Men, like Rooks to the Gamesters, who only fill a room at the Table, but are so far from contributing to the play, that they only serve to spoil the fancy of those that do.

DORILANT

Nay, they are us'd like Rooks too, snub'd, check'd, and abus'd; yet the Rogues will hang on.

HORNER

A Pox on'em, and all that force Nature, and wou'd be still what she forbids'em; Affectation is her greatest Monster.

HARCOURT

Most Men are the contraries to that they wou'd seem; your bully you see, is a Coward with a long Sword; the little humbly fawning Physician with his Ebony cane, is he that destroys Men.

DORILANT

The Usurer, a poor Rogue, possess'd of moldy Bonds, and Mortgages; and we they call Spend-thrifts, are only wealthy, who lay out his money upon daily new purchases of pleasure.

HORNER

Ay, your errantest cheat, is your Trustee, or Executor; your jealous Man, the greatest Cuckhold; your Church-man, the greatest Atheist; and your noisy pert Rogue of a wit, the greatest Fop, dullest Ass, and worst Company as you shall see: For here he comes.

[Enter **SPARKISH** to them.

SPARKISH

How is't, Sparks, how is't? Well Faith, Harry, I must railly thee a little, ha, ha, ha, upon the report in Town of thee, ha, ha, ha, I can't hold y Faith; shall I speak?

HORNER

Yes, but you'l be so bitter then.

SPARKISH

Honest Dick and Franck here shall answer for me, I will not be extream bitter by the Univers.

HARCOURT

We will be bound in ten thousand pound Bond, he shall not be bitter at all.

DORILANT

Nor sharp, nor sweet.

HORNER
What, not down right insipid?

SPARKISH
Nay then, since you are so brisk, and provoke me, take what follows; you must know, I was discoursing and raillying with some Ladies yesterday, and they hapned to talk of the fine new signes in Town.

HORNER
Very fine Ladies I believe.

SPARKISH
Said I, I know where the best new sign is. Where, says one of the Ladies? In Covent-Garden, I reply'd. Said another, In what street? In Russel-street, answer'd I. Lord says another, I'm sure there was ne're a fine new sign there yesterday. Yes, but there was, said I again, and it came out of France, and has been there a fortnight.

DORILANT
A Pox I can hear no more, prethee.

HORNER
No hear him out; let him tune his crowd a while.

HARCOURT
The worst Musick the greatest preparation.

SPARKISH
Nay faith, I'll make you laugh. It cannot be, says a third Lady. Yes, yes, quoth I again. Says a fourth Lady,

HORNER
Look to't, we'l have no more Ladies.

SPARKISH
No.—then mark, mark, now, said I to the fourth, did you never see Mr. Horner; he lodges in Russel-street, and he's a sign of a Man, you know, since he came out of France, heh, hah, he.

HORNER
But the Divel take me, is thine be the sign of a jest.

SPARKISH
With that they all fell a laughing, till they bepiss'd themselves; what, but it do's not move you, methinks? well see one had as good go to Law without a witness, as break a jest without a laugher on ones side.—Come, come Sparks, but where do we dine, I have left at Whitehal an Earl to dine with you.

DORILANT
Why, I thought thou hadst lov'd a Man with a title better, than a Suit with a French trimming to't.

HARCOURT
Go, to him again.

SPARKISH
No, Sir, a wit to me is the greatest title in the World.

HORNER
But go dine with your Earl, Sir, he may be exceptious; we are your Friends, and will not take it ill to be left, I do assure you.

HARCOURT
Nay, faith he shall go to him.

SPARKISH
Nay, pray Gentlemen.

DORILANT
We'l thrust you out, if you wo'not, what disappoint any Body for us.

SPARKISH
Nay, dear Gentlemen hear me.

HORNER
No, no, Sir, by no means; pray go Sir.

SPARKISH
Why, dear Rogues.

[They all thrust him out of the room.

DORILANT
No, no.

ALL
Ha, ha, ha.

[**SPARKISH** returns.

SPARKISH
But, Sparks, pray hear me; what d'ye think I'll eat then with gay shallow Fops, and silent Coxcombs? I think wit as necessary at dinner as a glass of good wine, and that's the reason I never have any stomach when I eat alone.—Come, but where do we dine?

HORNER
Ev'n where you will.

SPARKISH
At Chateline's.

DORILANT
Yes, if you will.

SPARKISH
Or at the Cock.

DORILANT
Yes, if you please.

SPARKISH
Or at the Dog and Partridg.

HORNER
Ay, if you have mind to't, for we shall dine at neither.

SPARKISH
Pshaw, with your fooling we shall loose the new Play; and I wou'd no more miss seing a new Play the first day, than I wou'd miss setting in the wits Row; therefore I'll go fetch my Mistriss and away.

[Exit **SPARKISH**.

[Manent **HORNER, HARCOURT, DORILANT**; Enter to them **MR PINCHWIFE**.

HORNER
Who have we here, Pinchwife?

MR PINCHWIFE
Gentlemen, your humble Servant.

HORNER
Well, Jack, by thy long absence from the Town, the grumness of thy countenance, and the slovenlyness of thy habit; I shou'd give thee joy, shoud' I not, of Marriage?

MR PINCHWIFE
Death does he know I'm married too? I thought to have conceal'd it from him at least. [Aside. My long stay in the Country will excuse my dress, and I have a suit of Law, that brings me up to Town, that puts me out of humour; besides I must give Sparkish to morrow five thousand pound to lye with my Sister.

HORNER
Nay, you Country Gentlemen rather than not purchase, will buy any thing, and he is a crackt title, if we may quibble: Well, but am I to give thee joy, I heard thou wert marry'd.

MR PINCHWIFE
What then?

HORNER
Why, the next thing that is to be heard, is thou'rt a Cuckold.

MR PINCHWIFE
Insupportable name.

[Aside.

HORNER
But I did not expect Marriage from such a Whoremaster as you, one that knew the Town so much, and Women so well.

MR PINCHWIFE
Why, I have marry'd no London Wife.

HORNER
Pshaw, that's all one, that grave circumspection in marrying a Country Wife, is like refusing a deceitful pamper'd Smithfield Jade, to go and be cheated by a Friend in the Country.

MR PINCHWIFE [Aside.
A Pox on him and his Simile. At least we are a little surer of the breed there, know what her keeping has been, whether foyl'd or unsound.

HORNER
Come, come, I have known a clap gotten in Wales, and there are Cozens, Justices, Clarks, and Chaplains in the Country, I won't say Coach-men, but she's handsome and young.

MR PINCHWIFE
I'll answer as I shou'd do. [Aside.
No, no, she has no beauty, but her youth; no attraction, but here modesty, wholesome, homely, and huswifely, that's all.

DORILANT
He talks as like a Grasier as he looks.

MR PINCHWIFE
She's too auker'd, ill favour'd, and silly to bring to Town.

HARCOURT
Then methinks you shou'd bring her, to be taught breeding.

MR PINCHWIFE
To be taught; no, Sir, I thank you, good Wives, and private Souldiers shou'd be ignorant.—I'll keep her from your instructions, I warrant you.

HARCOURT
The Rogue is as jealous, as if his wife were not ignorant. [Aside.

HORNER

Why, if she be ill favour'd, there will be less danger here for you, than by leaving her in the Country; we have such variety of dainties, that we are seldom hungry.

DORILANT
But they have alwayes coarse, constant, swinging stomachs in the Country.

HARCOURT
Foul Feeders indeed.

DORILANT
And your Hospitality is great there.

HARCOURT
Open house, every Man's welcome.

MR PINCHWIFE
So, so, Gentlemen.

HORNER
But prethee, why woud'st thou marry her? if she be ugly, ill bred, and silly, she must be rich then.

MR PINCHWIFE
As rich as if she brought me twenty thousand pound out of this Town; for she'l be as sure not to spend her moderate portion, as a London Baggage wou'd be to spend hers, let it be what it wou'd; so 'tis all one: then because shes ugly, she's the likelyer to be my own; and being ill bred, she'l hate conversation; and since silly and innocent, will not know the difference betwixt a Man of one and twenty, and one of forty

HORNER
Nine—to my knowledge; but if she be silly, she'l expect as much from a Man of forty nine, as from him of one and twenty: But methinks wit is more necessary than beauty, and I think no young Woman ugly that has it, and no handsome Woman agreable without it.

MR PINCHWIFE
'Tis my maxime, he's a Fool that marrys, but he's a greater that does not marry a Fool; what is wit in a Wife good for, but to make a Man a Cuckold?

HORNER
Yes, to keep it from his knowledge.

MR PINCHWIFE
A Fool cannot contrive to make her husband a Cuckold.

HORNER
No, but she'l club with a Man that can; and what is worse, if she cannot make her Husband a Cuckold, she'l make him jealous, and pass for one, and then 'tis all one.

MR PINCHWIFE

Well, well, I'll take care for one, my Wife shall make me no Cuckold, though she had your help Mr. Horner; I understand the Town, Sir.

DORILANT
His help! [Aside.

HARCOURT
He's come newly to Town it seems, and has not heard how things are with him. [Aside.

HORNER
But tell me, has Marriage cured thee of whoring, which it seldom does.

HARCOURT
'Tis more than age can do.

HORNER
No, the word is, I'll marry and live honest; but a Marriage vow is like a penitent Gamesters Oath, and entring into Bonds, and penalties to stint himself to such a particular small sum at play for the future, which makes him but the more eager, and not being able to hold out, looses his Money again, and his forfeit to boot.

DORILANT
Ay, ay, a Gamester will be a Gamester, whilst his Money lasts; and a Whoremaster, whilst his vigour.

HARCOURT
Nay, I have known'em, when they are broke and can loose no more, keep a fumbling with the Box in their hands to fool with only, and hinder other Gamesters.

DORILANT
That had wherewithal to make lusty stakes.

MR PINCHWIFE
Well, Gentlemen, you may laugh at me, but you shall never lye with my Wife, I know the Town.

HORNER
But prethee, was not the way you were in better, is not keeping better than Marriage?

MR PINCHWIFE
A Pox on't, the Jades wou'd jilt me, I cou'd never keep a Whore to my self.

HORNER
So then you only marry'd to keep a Whore to your self; well, but let me tell you, Women, as you say, are like Souldiers made constant and loyal by good pay, rather than by Oaths and Covenants, therefore I'd advise my Friends to keep rather than marry; since too I find by your example, it does not serve ones turn, for I saw you yesterday in the eighteen penny place with a pretty Country-wench.

MR PINCHWIFE

How the Divel, did he see my Wife then? I sate there that she might not be seen; but she shall never go to a play again. [Aside.

HORNER
What dost thou blush at nine and forty, for having been seen with a Wench?

DORILANT
No Faith, I warrant 'twas his Wife, which he seated there out of sight, for he's a cunning Rogue, and understands the Town.

HARCOURT
He blushes, then 'twas his Wife; for Men are now more ashamed to be seen with them in publick, than with a Wench.

MR PINCHWIFE
Hell and damnation, I'm undone, since Horner has seen her, and they know 'twas she. [Aside.

HORNER
But prethee, was it thy Wife? she was exceedingly pretty; I was in love with her at that distance.

MR PINCHWIFE
You are like never to be nearer to her. Your Servant Gentlemen.

[Offers to go.

HORNER
Nay, prethee stay.

MR PINCHWIFE
I cannot, I will not.

HORNER
Come you shall dine with us.

MR PINCHWIFE
I have din'd already.

HORNER
Come, I know thou hast not; I'll treat thee dear Rogue, thou sha't spend none of thy Hampshire Money to day.

MR PINCHWIFE
Treat me; so he uses me already like his Cuckold. [Aside.

HORNER
Nay, you shall not go.

MR PINCHWIFE

I must, I have business at home.

[Exit **MR PINCHWIFE**.

HARCOURT
To beat his Wife, he's as jealous of her, as a Cheapside Husband of a Covent-garden Wife.

HORNER
Why, 'tis as hard to find an old Whoremaster without jealousy and the gout, as a young one without fear or the Pox.

As Gout in Age, from Pox in Youth proceeds;
So Wenching past, then jealousy succeeds:
The worst disease that Love and Wenching breeds.

ACT II

SCENE I

MRS MARGERY PINCHWIFE, and **ALITHEA**: **MR PINCHWIFE** peeping behind at the door.

MRS PINCHWIFE
Pray, Sister, where are the best Fields and Woods, to walk in in London?

ALITHEA
A pretty Question; why, Sister! Mulberry Garden, and St. James's Park; and for close walks the New Exchange.

MRS PINCHWIFE
Pray, Sister, tell me why my Husband looks so grum here in Town? and keeps me up so close, and will not let me go a walking, nor let me wear my best Gown yesterday?

ALITHEA
O he's jealous, Sister.

MRS PINCHWIFE
Jealous, what's that?

ALITHEA
He's afraid you shou'd love another Man.

MRS PINCHWIFE
How shou'd he be afraid of my loving another man, when he will not let me see any but himself.

ALITHEA
Did he not carry you yesterday to a Play?

MRS PINCHWIFE
Ay, but we sate amongst ugly People, he wou'd not let me come near the Gentry, who sate under us, so that I cou'd not see'em: He told me, none but naughty Women sate there, whom they tous'd and mous'd; but I wou'd have ventur'd for all that.

ALITHEA
But how did you like the Play?

MRS PINCHWIFE
Indeed I was aweary of the Play, but I lik'd hugeously the Actors; they are the goodlyest proper'st Men, Sister.

ALITHEA
O but you must not like the Actors, Sister.

MRS PINCHWIFE
Ay, how shou'd I help it, Sister? Pray, Sister, when my Husband comes in, will you ask leave for me to go a walking?

ALITHEA
A walking, hah, ha; Lord, a Country Gentlewomans leasure is the drudgery of a foot-post; and she requires as much airing as her Husbands Horses. [Aside.

[Enter **MR PINCHWIFE** to them.

But here comes your Husband; I'll ask, though I'm sure he'l not grant it.

MRS PINCHWIFE
He says he won't let me go abroad, for fear of catching the Pox.

ALITHEA
Fye, the small Pox you shou'd say.

MRS PINCHWIFE
Oh my dear, dear Bud, welcome home; why dost thou look so fropish, who has nanger'd thee?

MR PINCHWIFE
Your a Fool.

[**MRS PINCHWIFE** goes aside, & cryes.

ALITHEA
Faith so she is, for crying for no fault, poor tender Creature!

MR PINCHWIFE
What you wou'd have her as impudent as your self, as errant a Jilflirt, a gadder, a Magpy, and to say all a meer notorious Town-Woman?

ALITHEA

Brother, you are my only Censurer; and the honour of your Family shall sooner suffer in your Wife there, than in me, though I take the innocent liberty of the Town.

MR PINCHWIFE

Hark you Mistriss, do not talk so before my Wife, the innocent liberty of the Town!

ALITHEA

Why, pray, who boasts of any intrigue with me? what Lampoon has made my name notorious? what ill Women frequent my Lodgings? I keep no Company with any Women of scandalous reputations.

MR PINCHWIFE

No, you keep the Men of scandalous reputations Company.

ALITHEA

Where? wou'd you not have me civil? answer'em in a Box at the Plays? in the drawing room at Whitehal? in St. James's Park? Mulberry-garden? or—

MR PINCHWIFE

Hold, hold, do not teach my Wife, where the Men are to be found; I believe she's the worse for your Town documents already; I bid you keep her in ignorance as I do.

MRS PINCHWIFE

Indeed be not angry with her Bud, she will tell me nothing of the Town, though I ask her a thousand times a day.

MR PINCHWIFE

Then you are very inquisitive to know, I find?

MRS PINCHWIFE

Not I indeed, Dear, I hate London; our Place-house in the Country is worth a thousand of't, wou'd I were there again.

MR PINCHWIFE

So you shall I warrant; but were you not talking of Plays, and Players, when I came in? you are her encourager in such discourses.

MRS PINCHWIFE

No indeed, Dear, she chid me just now for liking the Player Men.

MR PINCHWIFE

Nay, if she be so innocent as to own to me her lieking them, there is no hurt in't—[Aside. Come my poor Rogue, but thou lik'st none better then me?

MRS PINCHWIFE

Yes indeed, but I do, the Player Men are finer Folks.

MR PINCHWIFE
But you love none better then me?

MRS PINCHWIFE
You are mine own Dear Bud, and I know you, I hate a Stranger.

MR PINCHWIFE
Ay, my Dear, you must love me only, and not be like the naughty Town Women, who only hate their Husbands, and love every Man else, love Plays, Visits, fine Coaches, fine Cloaths, Fidles, Balls, Treates, and so lead a wicked Town-life.

MRS PINCHWIFE
Nay, if to enjoy all these things be a Town-life, London is not so bad a place, Dear.

MR PINCHWIFE
How! if you love me, you must hate London.

ALITHEA
The Fool has forbid me discovering to her the pleasures of the Town, and he is now setting her a gog upon them himself.

MRS PINCHWIFE
But, Husband, do the Town-women love the Player Men too?

MR PINCHWIFE
Yes, I warrant you.

MRS PINCHWIFE
Ay, I warrant you.

MR PINCHWIFE
Why, you do not, I hope?

MRS PINCHWIFE
No, no Bud; but why have we no Player-men in the Country?

MR PINCHWIFE
Ha—Mrs. Minx, ask me no more to go to a Play.

MRS PINCHWIFE
Nay, why, Love? I did not care for going; but when you forbid me, you make me as't were desire it.

ALITHEA
So 'twill be in other things, I warrant. [Aside.

MRS PINCHWIFE
Pray, let me go to a Play, Dear.

MR PINCHWIFE
Hold your Peace, I wo'not.

MRS PINCHWIFE
Why, Love?

MR PINCHWIFE
Why, I'll tell you.

ALITHEA
Nay, if he tell her, she'l give him more cause to forbid her that place. [Aside.

MRS PINCHWIFE
Pray, why, Dear?

MR PINCHWIFE
First, you like the Actors, and the Gallants may like you.

MRS PINCHWIFE
What, a homely Country Girl? no Bud, no body will like me.

MR PINCHWIFE
I tell you, yes, they may.

MRS PINCHWIFE
No, no, you jest—I won't believe you, I will go.

MR PINCHWIFE
I tell you then, that one of the lewdest Fellows in Town, who saw you there, told me he was in love with you.

MRS PINCHWIFE
Indeed! who, who, pray who wast?

MR PINCHWIFE
I've gone too far, and slipt before I was aware; how overjoy'd she is! [Aside.

MRS PINCHWIFE
Was it any Hampshire Gallant, any of our Neighbours? I promise you, I am beholding to him.

MR PINCHWIFE
I promise you, you lye; for he wou'd but ruin you, as he has done hundreds: he has no other love for Women, but that, such as he, look upon Women like Basilicks, but to destroy'em.

MRS PINCHWIFE
Ay, but if he loves me, why shou'd he ruin me? answer me to that: methinks he shou'd not, I wou'd do him no harm.

ALITHEA
Hah, ha, ha.

MR PINCHWIFE
'Tis very well; but I'll keep him from doing you any harm, or me either.

[Enter **SPARKISH** and **HARCOURT**.

But here comes Company, get you in, get you in.

MRS PINCHWIFE
But pray, Husband, is he a pretty Gentleman, that loves me?

MR PINCHWIFE
In baggage, in.

[Thrusts her in: shuts the door.

What all the lewd Libertines of the Town brought to my Lodging, by this easie Coxcomb! S'death I'll not suffer it.

SPARKISH
Here Harcourt, do you approve my choice? Dear, little Rogue, I told you, I'd bring you acquainted with all my Friends, the wits, and—

[**HARCOURT** salutes her.

MR PINCHWIFE
Ay, they shall know her, as well as you your self will, I warrant you.

SPARKISH
This is one of those, my pretty Rogue, that are to dance at your Wedding to morrow; and him you must bid welcom ever, to what you and I have.

MR PINCHWIFE
Monstrous!—[Aside.

SPARKISH
Harcourt how dost thou like her, Faith? Nay, Dear, do not look down; I should hate to have a Wife of mine out of countenance at any thing.

MR PINCHWIFE
Wonderful!

SPARKISH
Tell me, I say, Harcourt, how dost thou like her? thou hast star'd upon her enough, to resolve me.

HARCOURT

So infinitely well, that I cou'd wish I had a Mistriss too, that might differ from her in nothing, but her love and engagement to you.

ALITHEA
Sir, Master Sparkish has often told me, that his Acquaintance were all Wits and Raillieurs, and now I find it.

SPARKISH
No, by the Universe, Madam, he does not railly now; you may believe him: I do assure you, he is the honestest, worthyest, true hearted Gentleman—A man of such perfect honour, he wou'd say nothing to a Lady, he does not mean.

MR PINCHWIFE
Praising another Man to his Mistriss!

HARCOURT
Sir, you are so beyond expectation obliging, that—

SPARKISH
Nay, I gad, I am sure you do admire her extreamly, I see't in your eyes.—He does admire you Madam.—By the World, don't you?

HARCOURT
Yes, above the World, or, the most glorious part of it, her whole Sex; and till now I never thought I shou'd have envy'd you, or any Man about to marry, but you have the best excuse for Marriage I ever knew.

ALITHEA
Nay, now, Sir, I'm satisfied you are of the Society of the Wits, and Raillieurs, since you cannot spare your Friend, even when he is but too civil to you; but the surest sign is, since you are an Enemy to Marriage, for that I hear you hate as much as business or bad Wine.

HARCOURT
Truly, Madam, I never was an Enemy to Marriage, till now, because Marriage was never an Enemy to me before.

ALITHEA
But why, Sir, is Marriage an Enemy to you now? Because it robs you of your Friend here; for you look upon a Friend married, as one gone into a Monastery, that is dead to the World.

HARCOURT
'Tis indeed, because you marry him; I see Madam, you can guess my meaning: I do confess heartily and openly, I wish it were in my power to break the Match, by Heavens I wou'd.

SPARKISH
Poor Franck!

ALITHEA

Wou'd you be so unkind to me?

HARCOURT
No, no, 'tis not because I wou'd be unkind to you.

SPARKISH
Poor Franck, no gad, 'tis only his kindness to me.

MR PINCHWIFE
Great kindness to you indeed; insensible Fop, let a Man make love to his Wife to his face. [Aside.

SPARKISH
Come dear Franck, for all my Wife there that shall be, thou shalt enjoy me sometimes dear Rogue; by my honour, we Men of wit condole for our deceased Brother in Marriage, as much as for one dead in earnest: I think that was prettily said of me, ha Harcourt?—But come Franck, he not not melancholy for me.

HARCOURT
No, I assure you I am not melancholy for you.

SPARKISH
Prethee, Frank, dost think my Wife that shall be there a fine Person?

HARCOURT
I cou'd gaze upon her, till I became as blind as you are.

SPARKISH
How, as I am! how!

HARCOURT
Because you are a Lover, and true Lovers are blind, stockblind.

SPARKISH
True, true; but by the World, she has wit too, as well as beauty: go, go with her into a corner, and trye if she has wit, talk to her any thing, she's bashful before me.

HARCOURT
Indeed if a Woman wants wit in a corner, she has it no where.

ALITHEA
Sir, you dispose of me a little before your time.—[Aside to **SPARKISH**.

SPARKISH
Nay, nay, Madam let me have an earnest of your obedience, or—go, go, Madam—

[**HARCOURT** courts **ALITHEA** aside.

MR PINCHWIFE

How, Sir, if you are not concern'd for the honour of a wife, I am for that of a Sister; he shall not debauch her: be a Pander to your own wife, bring Men to her, let'em make love before your face, thrust'em into a corner together, then leav'em in private! is this your Town wit and conduct?

SPARKISH
Hah, ha, ha, a silly wise Rogue, wou'd make one laugh more then a stark Fool, hah, ha: I shall burst. Nay, you shall not disturb'em; I'll vex thee, by the World.

Struggles with **MR PINCHWIFE** *to keep, him from* **HARCOURT** *and* **ALITHEA**

ALITHEA
The writings are drawn, Sir, settlements made; 'tis too late, Sir, and past all revocation.

HARCOURT
Then so is my death.

ALITHEA
I wou'd not be unjust to him.

HARCOURT
Then why to me so?

ALITHEA
I have no obligation to you.

HARCOURT
My love.

ALITHEA
I had his before.

HARCOURT
You never had it; he wants you see jealousie, the only infallible sign of it.

ALITHEA
Love proceeds from esteem; he cannot distrust my virtue, besides he loves me, or he wou'd not marry me.

HARCOURT
Marrying you, is no more sign of his love, then bribing your Woman, that he may marry you, is a sign of his generosity: Marriage is rather a sign of interest, then love; and he that marries a fortune, covets a Mistress, not loves her: But if you take Marriage for a sign of love, take it from me immediately.

ALITHEA
No, now you have put a scruple in my head; but in short, Sir, to end our dispute, I must marry him, my reputation wou'd suffer in the World else.

HARCOURT

No, if you do marry him, with your pardon, Madam, your reputation suffers in the World, and you wou'd be thought in necessity for a cloak.

ALITHEA
Nay, now you are rude, Sir.—Mr. Sparkish, pray come hither, your Friend here is very troublesom, and very loving.

HARCOURT
Hold, hold—[Aside to **ALITHEA**.

MR PINCHWIFE
D'ye hear that?

SPARKISH
Why, d'ye think I'll seem to be jealous, like a Country Bumpkin?

MR PINCHWIFE
No, rather be a Cuckold, like a credulous Cit.

HARCOURT
Madam, you wou'd not have been so little generous as to have told him.

ALITHEA
Yes, since you cou'd be so little generous, as to wrong him.

HARCOURT
Wrong him, no Man can do't, he's beneath an injury; a Bubble, a Coward, a sensless Idiot, a Wretch so contemptible to all the World but you, that—

ALITHEA
Hold, do not rail at him, for since he is like to be my Husband, I am resolv'd to like him: Nay, I think I am oblig'd to tell him, you are not his Friend.—Master Sparkish, Master Sparkish.

SPARKISH
What, what; now dear Rogue, has not she wit?

HARCOURT
Not so much as I thought, and hoped she had. [Speaks surlily.

ALITHEA
Mr. Sparkish, do you bring People to rail at you?

HARCOURT
Madam—

SPARKISH
How! no, but if he does rail at me, 'tis but in jest I warrant; what we wits do for one another, and never take any notice of it.

ALITHEA

He spoke so scurrilously of you, I had no patience to hear him; besides he has been making love to me.

HARCOURT

True damn'd tell-tale-Woman. [Aside.

SPARKISH

Pshaw, to shew his parts—we wits rail and make love often, but to shew our parts; as we have no affections, so we have no malice, we—

ALITHEA

He said, you were a Wretch, below an injury.

SPARKISH

Pshaw.

HARCOURT

Damn'd, sensless, impudent, virtuous Jade; well since she won't let me have her, she'l do as good, she'l make me hate her.

ALITHEA

A Common Bubble.

SPARKISH

Pshaw.

ALITHEA

A Coward.

SPARKISH

Pshaw, pshaw.

ALITHEA

A sensless driveling Idiot.

SPARKISH

How, did he disparage my parts? Nay, then my honour's concern'd, I can't put up that, Sir; by the World, Brother help me to kill him; [Aside. [I may draw now, since we have the odds of him:—'tis a good occasion too before my Mistriss]—

[Offers to draw.

ALITHEA

Hold, hold.

SPARKISH

What, what.

ALITHEA
I must not let'em kill the Gentleman neither, for his kindness to me; I am so far from hating him, that I wish my Gallant had his person and understanding:—[Aside] Nay if my honour—

SPARKISH
I'll be thy death.

ALITHEA
Hold, hold, indeed to tell the truth, the Gentleman said after all, that what he spoke, was but out of friendship to you.

SPARKISH
How! say, I am, I am a Fool, that is no wit, out of friendship to me.

ALITHEA
Yes, to try whether I was concern'd enough for you, and made love to me only to be satisfy'd of my virtue, for your sake.

HARCOURT
Kind however—[Aside.

SPARKISH
Nay, if it were so, my dear Rogue, I ask thee pardon; but why wou'd not you tell me so, faith.

HARCOURT
Because I did not think on't, faith.

SPARKISH
Come, Horner does not come, Harcourt, let's be gone to the new Play.—Come Madam.

ALITHEA
I will not go, if you intend to leave me alone in the Box, and run into the pit, as you use to do.

SPARKISH
Pshaw, I'll leave Harcourt with you in the Box, to entertain you, and that's as good; if I sate in the Box, I shou'd be thought no Judge, but of trimmings.—Come away Harcourt, lead her down.

[Exeunt **SPARKISH, HARCOURT,** and **ALITHEA.**

MR PINCHWIFE
Well, go thy wayes, for the flower of the true Town Fops, such as spend their Estates, before they come to'em, and are Cuckolds before they'r married. But let me go look to my own Free-hold—How—

[Enter my **LADY FIDGET, MISTRISS FIDGET DAINTY FIDGET,** and **MISTRISS SQUEAMISH.**

LADY FIDGET
Your Servant, Sir, where is your Lady? we are come to wait upon her to the new Play.

MR PINCHWIFE
New Play!

LADY FIDGET
And my Husband will wait upon you presently.

MR PINCHWIFE
Damn your civility—[Aside. Madam, by no means, I will not see Sir Jaspar here, till I have waited upon him at home; nor shall my Wife see you, till she has waited upon your Ladyship at your lodgings.

LADY FIDGET
Now we are here, Sir—

MR PINCHWIFE
No, Madam.

MRS DAINTY FIDGET
Pray, let us see her.

MISTRISS SQUEAMISH
We will not stir, till we see her.

MR PINCHWIFE
A Pox on you all—[Aside.
Goes to the door, and returns.
she has lock'd the door, and is gone abroad.

LADY FIDGET
No, you have lock'd the door, and she's within.

MRS DAINTY FIDGET
They told us below, she was here.

MR PINCHWIFE
Will nothing do?—Well it must out then, to tell you the truth, Ladies, which I was afraid to let you know before, least it might endanger your lives, my Wife has just now the Small Pox come out upon her, do not be frighten'd; but pray, be gone Ladies, you shall not stay here in danger of your lives; pray get you gone Ladies.

LADY FIDGET
No, no, we have all had'em.

MISTRISS SQUEAMISH
Alack, alack.

MRS DAINTY FIDGET
Come, come, we must see how it goes with her, I understand the disease.

LADY FIDGET
Come.

MR PINCHWIFE
Well, there is no being too hard for Women at their own weapon, lying, therefore I'll quit the Field.
[Aside.

[Exit **MR PINCHWIFE**.

MISTRISS SQUEAMISH
Here's an example of jealousy.

LADY FIDGET
Indeed as the World goes, I wonder there are no more jealous, since Wives are so neglected.

MRS DAINTY FIDGET
Pshaw, as the World goes, to what end shou'd they be jealous.

LADY FIDGET
Foh, 'tis a nasty World.

MISTRISS SQUEAMISH
That Men of parts, great acquaintance, and quality shou'd take up with, and spend themselves and
fortunes, in keeping little Play-house Creatures, foh.

LADY FIDGET
Nay, that Women of understanding, great acquaintance, and good quality, shou'd fall a keeping too of
little Creatures, foh.

MISTRISS SQUEAMISH
Why, 'tis the Men of qualities fault, they never visit Women of honour, and reputation, as they us'd to
do; and have not so much as common civility, for Ladies of our rank, but use us with the same
indifferency, and ill breeding, as if we were all marry'd to'em.

LADY FIDGET
She says true, 'tis an errant shame Women of quality shou'd be so slighted; methinks, birth, birth, shou'd
go for something; I have known Men admired, courted, and followed for their titles only.

MISTRISS SQUEAMISH
Ay, one wou'd think Men of honour shou'd not love no more, than marry out of their own rank.

MRS DAINTY FIDGET
Fye, fye upon'em, they are come to think cross breeding for themselves best, as well as for their Dogs,
and Horses.

LADY FIDGET
They are Dogs, and Horses for't.

MISTRISS SQUEAMISH
One wou'd think if not for love, for vanity a little.

MRS DAINTY FIDGET
Nay, they do satisfy their vanity upon us sometimes; and are kind to us in their report, tell all the World they lye with us.

LADY FIDGET
Damn'd Rascals, that we shou'd be only wrong'd by'em; to report a Man has had a Person, when he has not had a Person, is the greatest wrong in the whole World, that can be done to a person.

MISTRISS SQUEAMISH
Well, 'tis an errant shame, Noble Persons shou'd be so wrong'd, and neglected.

LADY FIDGET
But still 'tis an erranter shame for a Noble Person, to neglect her own honour, and defame her own Noble Person, with little inconsiderable Fellows, foh!—

MRS DAINTY FIDGET
I suppose the crime against our honour, is the same with a Man of quality as with another.

LADY FIDGET
How! no sure the Man of quality is likest one's Husband, and therefore the fault shou'd be the less.

MRS DAINTY FIDGET
But then the pleasure shou'd be the less.

LADY FIDGET
Fye, fye, fye, for shame Sister, whither shall we ramble? be continent in your discourse, or I shall hate you.

MRS DAINTY FIDGET
Besides an intrigue is so much the more notorious for the man's quality.

MISTRISS SQUEAMISH
'Tis true, no body takes notice of a private Man, and therefore with him, 'tis more secret, and the crime's the less, when 'tis not known.

LADY FIDGET
You say true; y faith I think you are in the right on't: 'tis not an injury to a Husband, till it be an injury to our honours; so that a Woman of honour looses no honour with a private Person; and to say truth—

MRS DAINTY FIDGET
So the little Fellow is grown a private Person— with her—[Apart to **SQUEAMISH**.

LADY FIDGET
But still my dear, dear Honour.

[Enter **SIR JASPAR, HORNER, DORILANT**.

SIR JASPAR
Ay, my dear, dear of honour, thou hast still so much honour in thy mouth—

HORNER
That she has none elsewhere—[Aside.

LADY FIDGET
Oh, what d'ye mean to bring in these upon us?

MRS DAINTY FIDGET
Foh, these are as bad as Wits.

MISTRISS SQUEAMISH
Foh!

LADY FIDGET
Let us leave the Room.

SIR JASPAR
Stay, stay, faith to tell you the naked truth.

LADY FIDGET
Fye, Sir Jaspar, do not use that word naked.

SIR JASPAR
Well, well, in short I have business at Whitehal, and cannot go to the play with you, therefore wou'd have you go—

LADY FIDGET
With those two to a Play?

SIR JASPAR
No, not with t'other, but with Mr. Horner, there can be no more scandal to go with him, than with Mr. Tatle, or Master Limberham.

LADY FIDGET
With that nasty Fellow! no—no.

SIR JASPAR
Nay, prethee Dear, hear me.

[Whispers to **LADY FIDGET. HORNER, DORILANT** drawing near **MISTRISS SQUEAMISH**, and **MRS DAINTY FIDGET**.

HORNER

Ladies.

MRS DAINTY FIDGET
Stand off.

MISTRISS SQUEAMISH
Do not approach us.

MRS DAINTY FIDGET
You heard with the wits, you are obscenity all over.

MISTRISS SQUEAMISH
And I wou'd as soon look upon a Picture of Adam and Eve, without fig leaves, as any of you, if I cou'd help it, therefore keep off, and do not make us sick.

DORILANT
What a Divel are these?

HORNER
Why, these are pretenders to honour, as criticks to wit, only by censuring others; and as every raw peevish, out-of-humour'd, affected, dull, Tea-drinking, Arithmetical Fop sets up for a wit, by railing at men of sence, so these for honour, by railing at the Court, and Ladies of as great honour, as quality.

SIR JASPAR
Come, Mr. Horner, I must desire you to go with these Ladies to the Play, Sir.

HORNER
I! Sir.

SIR JASPAR
Ay, ay, come, Sir.

HORNER
I must-beg your pardon, Sir, and theirs, I will not be seen in Womens Company in publick again for the World.

SIR JASPAR
Ha, ha, strange Aversion!

MISTRISS SQUEAMISH
No, he's for Womens company in private.

SIR JASPAR
He—poor Man—he! hah, ha, ha.

MRS DAINTY FIDGET
'Tis a greater shame amongst lew'd fellows to be seen in virtuous Womens company, than for the Women to be seen with them.

HORNER
Indeed, Madam, the time was I only hated virtuous Women, but now I hate the other too; I beg your pardon Ladies.

LADY FIDGET
You are very obliging, Sir, because we wou'd not be troubled with you.

SIR JASPAR
In sober sadness he shall go.

DORILANT
Nay, if he wo'not, I am ready to wait upon the Ladies; and I think I am the fitter Man.

SIR JASPAR
You, Sir, no I thank you for that—Master Horner is a privileg'd Man amongst the virtuous Ladies, 'twill be a great while before you are so; heh, he, he, he's my Wive's Gallant, heh, he, he; no pray withdraw, Sir, for as I take it, the virtuous Ladies have no business with you.

DORILANT
And I am sure, he can have none with them: 'tis strange a Man can't come amongst virtuous Women now, but upon the same terms, as Men are admitted into the great Turks Seraglio; but Heavens keep me, from being an hombre Player with'em: but where is Pinchwife—

[Exit **DORILANT**.

SIR JASPAR
Come, come, Man; what avoid the sweet society of Woman-kind? that sweet, soft, gentle, tame, noble Creature Woman, made for Man's Companion—

HORNER
So is that soft, gentle, tame, and more noble Creature a Spaniel, and has all their tricks, can fawn, lye down, suffer beating, and fawn the more; barks at your Friends, when they come to see you; makes your bed hard, gives you Fleas, and the mange sometimes: and all the difference is, the Spaniel's the more faithful Animal, and fawns but upon one Master.

SIR JASPAR
Heh, he, he.

MISTRISS SQUEAMISH
O the rude Beast.

MRS DAINTY FIDGET
Insolent brute.

LADY FIDGET
Brute! stinking mortify'd rotten French Weather, to dare—

SIR JASPAR

Hold, an't please your Ladyship; for shame Master, Horner your Mother was a Woman—[Aside] Now shall I never reconcile'em. Hark you, Madam, take my advice in your anger; you know you often want one to make up your droling pack of hombre Players; and you may cheat him easily, for he's an ill Gamester, and consequently loves play: Besides you know, you have but two old civil Gentlemen (with stinking breaths too) to wait upon you abroad, take in the third, into your service; the other are but crazy: and a Lady shou'd have a supernumerary Gentleman-Usher, as a supernumerary Coach-horse, least sometimes you shou'd be forc'd to stay at home.

LADY FIDGET

But are you sure he loves play, and has money?

SIR JASPAR

He loves play as much as you, and has money as much as I.

LADY FIDGET

Then I am contented to make him pay for his scurrillity; money makes up in a measure all other wants in Men.— Those whom we cannot make hold for Gallants, we make fine. [Aside.

SIR JASPAR

So, so; now to mollify, to wheedle him,—[Aside]. Master Horner will you never keep civil Company, methinks 'tis time now, since you are only fit for them: Come, come, Man you must e'en fall to visiting our Wives, eating at our Tables, drinking Tea with our virtuous Relations after dinner, dealing Cards to'em, reading Plays, and Gazets to'em, picking Fleas out of their shocks for'em, collecting Receipts, New Songs, Women, Pages, and Footmen for'em.

HORNER

I hope they'l afford me better employment, Sir.

SIR JASPAR

Heh, he, he, 'tis fit you know your work before you come into your place; and since you are unprovided of a Lady to flatter, and a good house to eat at, pray frequent mine, and call my Wife Mistriss, and she shall call you Gallant, according to the custom.

HORNER

Who I?—

SIR JASPAR

Faith, thou sha't for my sake, come for my sake only.

HORNER

For your sake—

SIR JASPAR

Come, come, here's a Gamester for you, let him be a little familiar sometimes; nay, what if a little rude; Gamesters may be rude with Ladies, you know.

LADY FIDGET

Yes, losing Gamesters have a privilege with Women.

HORNER
I alwayes thought the contrary, that the winning Gamester had most privilege with Women, for when you have lost your money to a Man, you'l loose any thing you have, all you have, they say, and he may use you as he pleases.

SIR JASPAR
Heh, he, he, well, win or loose you shall have your liberty with her.

LADY FIDGET
As he behaves himself; and for your sake I'll give him admittance and freedom.

HORNER
All sorts of freedom, Madam?

SIR JASPAR
Ay, ay, ay, all forts of freedom thou can'st take, and so go to her, begin thy new employment; wheedle her, jest with her, and be better acquainted one with another.

HORNER
I think I know her already, therefore may venter with her, my secret for hers—[Aside.

HORNER, and **LADY FIDGET** whisper.

SIR JASPAR
Sister Cuz, I have provided an innocent Play-fellow for you there.

MRS DAINTY FIDGET
Who he!

MISTRISS SQUEAMISH
There's a Play-fellow indeed.

SIR JASPAR
Yes sure, what he is good enough to play at Cards, Blind-mans buff, or the fool with sometimes.

MISTRISS SQUEAMISH
Foh, we'l have no such Play-fellows.

MRS DAINTY FIDGET
No, Sir, you shan't choose Play-fellows for us, we thank you.

SIR JASPAR
Nay, pray hear me.

[Whispering to them.

LADY FIDGET

But, poor Gentleman, cou'd you be so generous? so truly a Man of honour, as for the sakes of us Women of honour, to cause your self to be reported no Man? No Man! and to suffer your self the greatest shame that cou'd fall upon a Man, that none might fall upon us Women by your conversation; but indeed, Sir, as perfectly, perfectly, the same Man as before your going into France, Sir; as perfectly, perfectly, Sir.

HORNER

As perfectly, perfectly, Madam; nay, I scorn you shou'd take my word; I desire to be try'd only, Madam.

LADY FIDGET

Well, that's spoken again like a Man of honour, all Men of honour desire to come to the test: But indeed, generally you Men report such things of your selves, one does not know how, or whom to believe; and it is come to that pass, we dare not take your words, no more than your Taylors, without some staid Servant of yours be bound with you; but I have so strong a faith in your honour, dear, dear, noble Sir, that I'd forfeit mine for yours at any time, dear Sir.

HORNER

No, Madam, you shou'd not need to forfeit it for me, I have given you security already to save you harmless my late reputation being so well known in the World, Madam.

LADY FIDGET

But if upon any future falling out, or upon a suspition of my taking the trust out of your hands, to employ some other, you your self shou'd betray your trust, dear Sir; I mean, if you'l give me leave to speak obscenely, you might tell, dear Sir.

HORNER

If I did, no body wou'd believe me; the reputation of impotency is as hardly recover'd again in the World, as that of cowardise, dear Madam.

LADY FIDGET

Nay then, as one may say, you may do your worst, dear, dear, Sir.

SIR JASPAR

Come, is your Ladyship reconciled to him yet? have you agreed on matters? for I must be gone to Whitehal.

LADY FIDGET

Why, indeed, Sir Jaspar, Master Horner is a thousand, thousand times a better Man, than I thought him: Cosen Squeamish, Sister Dainty, I can name him now, truly not long ago you know, I thought his very name obscenity, and I wou'd as soon have lain with him, as have nam'd him.

SIR JASPAR

Very likely, poor Madam.

MRS DAINTY FIDGET

I believe it.

MISTRISS SQUEAMISH
No doubt on't.

SIR JASPAR
Well, well—that your Ladyship is as virtuous as any she,—I know, and him all the Town knows—heh, he, he; therefore now you like him, get you gone to your business together; go, go, to your business, I say, pleasure, whilst I go to my pleasure, business.

LADY FIDGET
Come than dear Gallant.

HORNER
Come away, my dearest Mistriss.

SIR JASPAR
So, so, why 'tis as I'd have it.

[Exit **SIR JASPAR**.

HORNER
And as I'd have it.

LADY FIDGET
Who for his business, from his Wife will run;
Takes the best care, to have her bus'ness done.

[Exeunt **OMNES**.

ACT III

SCENE I

ALITHEA, and **MRS PINCHWIFE**.

ALITHEA
Sister, what ailes you, you are grown melancholy?

MRS PINCHWIFE
Wou'd it not make any one melancholy, to see you go every day fluttering about abroad, whil'st I must stay at home like a poor lonely, sullen Bird in a cage?

ALITHEA
Ay, Sister, but you came young, and just from the nest to your cage, so that I thought you lik'd it; and cou'd be as chearful in't, as others that took their flight themselves early, and are hopping abroad in the open Air.

MRS PINCHWIFE

Nay, I confess I was quiet enough, till my Husband told me, what pure lives, the London Ladies live abroad, with their dancing, meetings, and junketings, and drest every day in their best gowns; and I warrant you, play at nine Pins every day of the week, so they do.

[Enter **MR PINCHWIFE**.

MR PINCHWIFE

Come, what's here to do? you are putting the Town pleasures in her head, and setting her a longing.

ALITHEA

Yes, after Nine-pins; you suffer none to give her those longings, you mean, but your self.

MR PINCHWIFE

I tell her of the vanities of the Town like a Confessor.

ALITHEA

A Confessor! just such a Confessor, as he that by forbidding a silly Oastler to grease the Horses teeth, taught him to do't.

MR PINCHWIFE

Come Mistriss Flippant, good Precepts are lost, when bad Examples are still before us; the liberty you take abroad makes her hanker after it; and out of humour at home, poor Wretch! she desired not to come to London, I wou'd bring her.

ALITHEA

Very well.

MR PINCHWIFE

She has been this week in Town, and never desired, till this afternoon, to go abroad.

ALITHEA

Was she not at a Play yesterday?

MR PINCHWIFE

Yes, but she ne'er ask'd me; I was my self the cause of her going.

ALITHEA

Then if she ask you again, you are the cause of her asking, and not my example.

MR PINCHWIFE

Well, to morrow night I shall be rid of you; and the next day before 'tis light, she and I'll be rid of the Town, and my dreadful apprehensions: Come, be not melancholly, for thou sha't go into the Country after to morrow, Dearest.

ALITHEA

Great comfort.

MRS PINCHWIFE
Pish, what d'ye tell me of the Country for?

MR PINCHWIFE
How's this! what, pish at the Country?

MRS PINCHWIFE
Let me alone, I am not well.

MR PINCHWIFE
O, if that be all—what ailes my dearest?

MRS PINCHWIFE
Truly I don't know; but I have not been well, since you told me there was a Gallant at the Play in love with me.

MR PINCHWIFE
Ha—

ALITHEA
That's by my example too.

MR PINCHWIFE
Nay, if you are not well, but are so concern'd, because a lew'd Fellow chanc'd to lye, and say he lik'd you, you'l make me sick too.

MRS PINCHWIFE
Of what sickness?

MR PINCHWIFE
O, of that which is worse than the Plague, Jealousy.

MRS PINCHWIFE
Pish, you jear, I'm sure there's no such disease in our Receipt-book at home.

MR PINCHWIFE
No, thou never met'st with it, poor Innocent— well, if thou Cuckold me, 'twill be my own fault— for Cuckolds and Bastards, are generally makers of their own fortune. [Aside.

MRS PINCHWIFE
Well, but pray Bud, let's go to a Play to night.

MR PINCHWIFE
'Tis just done, she comes from it; but why are you so eager to see a Play?

MRS PINCHWIFE
Faith Dear, not that I care one pin for their talk there; but I like to look upon the Player-men, and wou'd see, if I cou'd, the Gallant you say loves me; that's all dear Bud.

MR PINCHWIFE
Is that all dear Bud?

ALITHEA
This proceeds from my example.

MRS PINCHWIFE
But if the Play be done, let's go abroad however, dear Bud.

MR PINCHWIFE
Come have a little patience, and thou shalt go into the Country on Friday.

MRS PINCHWIFE
Therefore I wou'd see first some sights, to tell my Neighbours of. Nay, I will go abroad, that's once.

ALITHEA
I'm the cause of this desire too.

MR PINCHWIFE
But now I think on't, who was the cause of Horners coming to my Lodging to day? that was you.

ALITHEA
No, you, because you wou'd not let him see your handsome Wife out of your Lodging.

MRS PINCHWIFE
Why, O Lord! did the Gentleman come hither to see me indeed?

MR PINCHWIFE
No, no;—You are not cause of that damn'd question too, Mistriss Alithea?—[Aside]. Well she's in the right of it; he is in love with my Wife—and comes after her— 'tis so—but I'll nip his love in the bud; least he should follow us into the Country, and break his Chariot-wheel near our house, on purpose for an excuse to come to't; but I think I know the Town.

MRS PINCHWIFE
Come, pray Bud, let's go abroad before 'tis late; for I will go, that's flat and plain.

MR PINCHWIFE
So! the obstinacy already of a Town-wife, and I must, whilst she's here, humour her like one. [Aside]. Sister, how shall we do, that she may not be seen, or known?

ALITHEA
Let her put on her Mask.

MR PINCHWIFE
Pshaw, a Mask makes People but the more inquisitive, and is as ridiculous a disguise, as a stage-beard; her shape, stature, habit will be known: and if we shou'd meet with Horner, he wou'd be sure to take acquaintance with us, must wish her joy, kiss her, talk to her, leer upon her, and the Devil and all; no I'll

not use her to a Mask, 'tis dangerous; for Masks have made more Cuckolds, than the best faces that ever were known.

ALITHEA
How will you do then?

MRS PINCHWIFE
Nay, shall we go? the Exchange will be shut, and I have a mind to see that.

MR PINCHWIFE
So—I have it—I'll dress her up in the Suit, we are to carry down to her Brother, little Sir James; nay, I understand the Town tricks: Come let's go dress her; a Mask! no—a Woman mask'd, like a cover'd Dish, gives a Man curiosity, and appetite, when, it may be, uncover'd, 'twou'd turn his stomack; no, no.

ALITHEA
Indeed your comparison is something a greasie one: but I had a gentle Gallant, us'd to say, a Beauty mask'd, lik'd the Sun in Eclipse, gathers together more gazers, than if it shin'd out.

[Exeunt.

THE SCENE CHANGES TO THE NEW EXCHANGE

Enter **HORNER, HARCOURT, DORILANT**.

DORILANT
Engag'd to Women, and not Sup with us?

HORNER
Ay, a Pox on'em all.

HARCOURT
You were much a more reasonable Man in the morning, and had as noble resolutions against'em, as a Widdower of a weeks liberty.

DORILANT
Did I ever think, to see you keep company with Women in vain.

HORNER
In vain! no—'tis, since I can't love'em, to be reveng'd on'em.

HARCOURT
Now your Sting is gone, you look'd in the Box amongst all those Women, like a drone in the hive, all upon you; shov'd and ill-us'd by'em all, and thrust from one side to t'other.

DORILANT

Yet he must be buzzing amongst'em still, like other old beetle-headed, lycorish drones; avoid'em, and hate'm as they hate you.

HORNER
Because I do hate'em, and wou'd hate'em yet more, I'll frequent'em; you may see by Marriage, nothing makes a Man hate a Woman more, than her constant conversation: In short, I converse with'em, as you do with rich Fools; to laugh at'em, and use'em ill.

DORILANT
But I wou'd no more Sup with Women, unless I cou'd lye with'em, than Sup with a rich Coxcomb, unless I cou'd cheat him.

HORNER
Yes, I have known thee Sup with a Fool, for his drinking, if he cou'd set out your hand that way only, you were satisfy'd; and if he were a Wine-swallowing mouth 'twas enough.

HARCOURT
Yes, a Man drink's often with a Fool, as he tosses with a Marker, only to keep his hand in Ure; but do the Ladies drink?

HORNER
Yes, Sir, and I shall have the pleasure at least of laying'em flat with a Bottle; and bring as much scandal that way upon'em, as formerly t'other.

HARCOURT
Perhaps you may prove as weak a Brother amongst'em that way, as t'other.

DORILANT
Foh, drinking with Women, is as unnatural, as scolding with'em; but 'tis a pleasure of decay'd Fornicators, and the basest way of quenching Love.

HARCOURT
Nay, 'tis drowning Love, instead of quenching it; but leave us for civil Women too!

DORILANT
Ay, when he can't be the better for'em; we hardly pardon a Man, that leaves his Friend for a Wench, and that's a pretty lawful call.

HORNER
Faith, I wou'd not leave you for'em, if they wou'd not drink.

DORILANT
Who wou'd disappoint his Company at Lewis's, for a Gossiping?

HARCOURT
Foh, Wine and Women good apart, together as nauseous as Sack and Sugar: But hark you, Sir, before you go, a little of your advice, an old maim'd General, when unfit for action is fittest for Counsel; I have

other designs upon Women, than eating and drinking with them: I am in love with Sparkish's Mistriss, whom he is to marry to morrow, now how shall I get her?

[Enter **SPARKISH**, looking about.

HORNER
Why, here comes one will help you to her.

HARCOURT
He! he, I tell you, is my Rival, and will hinder my love.

HORNER
No, a foolish Rival, and a jealous Husband assist their Rivals designs; for they are sure to make their Women hate them, which is the first step to their love, for another Man.

HARCOURT
But I cannot come near his Mistriss, but in his company.

HORNER
Still the better for you, for Fools are most easily cheated, when they themselves are accessaries; and he is to be bubled of his Mistriss, as of his Money, the common Mistriss, by keeping him company.

SPARKISH
Who is that, that is to be bubled? Faith let me snack, I han't met with a buble since Christmas: gad; I think bubles are like their Brother Woodcocks, go out with the cold weather.

HARCOURT
A Pox, he did not hear all I hope.

[Apart to **HORNER**.

SPARKISH
Come, you bubling Rogues you, where do we sup—Oh, Harcourt, my Mistriss tells me, you have been making fierce love to her all the Play long, hah, ha— but I—

HARCOURT
I make love to her?

SPARKISH
Nay, I forgive thee; for I think I know thee, and I know her, but I am sure I know my self.

HARCOURT
Did she tell you so? I see all Women are like these of the Fxchange, who to enhance the price of their commodities, report to their fond Customers offers which were never made'em.

HORNER

Ay, Women are as apt to tell before the intrigue, as Men after it, and so shew themselves the vainer Sex; but hast thou a Mistriss, Sparkish? 'tis as hard for me to believe it, as that thou ever hadst a buble, as you brag'd just now.

SPARKISH

O your Servant, Sir; are you at your raillery, Sir? but we were some of us beforehand with you to day at the Play: the Wits were something bold with you, Sir; did you not hear us laugh?

HARCOURT

Yes, But I thought you had gone to Plays, to laugh at the Poets wit, not at your own.

SPARKISH

Your Servant, Sir, no I thank you; gad I go to a Play as to a Country-treat, I carry my own wine to one, and my own wit to t'other, or else I'm sure I shou'd not be merry at either; and the reason why we are so often lowder, than the Players, is, because we think we speak more wit, and so become the Poets Rivals in his audience: for to tell you the truth, we hate the silly Rogues; nay, so much that we find fault even with their Bawdy upon the Stage, whilst we talk nothing else in the Pit as lowd.

HORNER

But, why should'st thou hate the silly Poets, thou hast too much wit to be one, and they like Whores are only hated by each other; and thou dost scorn writing, I'am sure.

SPARKISH

Yes, I'd have you to know, I scorn writing; but Women, Women, that make Men do all foolish things, make'em write Songs too; every body does it: 'tis ev'n as common with Lovers, as playing with fans; and you can no more help Rhyming to your Phyllis, than drinking to your Phyllis.

HARCOURT

Nay, Poetry in love is no more to be avoided, than jealousy.

DORILANT

But the Poets damn'd your Songs, did they?

SPARKISH

Damn the Poets, they turn'd'em into Burlesque, as they call it; that Burlesque is a Hocus-Pocus-trick, they have got, which by the virtue of Hictius doctius, topsey turvey, they make a wise and witty Man in the World, a Fool upon the Stage you know not how; and 'tis therefore I hate'em too, for I know not but it may be my own case; for they'l put a Man into a Play for looking a Squint: Their Predecessors were contented to make Serving-men only their Stage-Fools, but these Rogues must have Gentlemen, with a Pox to'em, nay Knights: and indeed you shall hardly see a Fool upon the Stage, but he's a Knight; and to tell you the truth, they have kept me these six years from being a Knight in earnest, for fear of being knighted in a Play, and dubb'd a Fool.

DORILANT

Blame'em not, they must follow their Copy, the Age.

HARCOURT

But why should'st thou be afraid of being in a Play, who expose your self every day in the Play-houses, and as publick Places.

HORNER
'Tis but being on the Stage, instead of standing on a Bench in the Pit.

DORILANT
Don't you give money to Painters to draw you like? and are you afraid of your Pictures, at length in a Play-house, where all your Mistresses may see you.

SPARKISH
A Pox, Painters don't draw the Small Pox, or Pimples in ones face; come damn all your silly Authors whatever, all Books and Booksellers, by the World, and all Readers, courteous or uncourteous.

HARCOURT
But, who comes here, Sparkish?

[Enter **MR PINCHWIFE**, and his **WIFE** in Mans Cloaths, **ALITHEA**, **LUCY** her Maid.

SPARKISH
Oh hide me, there's my Mistriss too.

SPARKISH hides himself behind **HARCOURT**.

HARCOURT
She sees you.

SPARKISH
But I will not see her, 'tis time to go to Whitehal, and I must not fail the drawing Room.

HARCOURT
Pray, first carry me, and reconcile me to her.

SPARKISH
Another time, faith the King will have sup't.

HARCOURT
Not with the worse stomach for thy absence; thou art one of those Fools, that think their attendance at the King's Meals, as necessary as his Physicians, when you are more troublesom to him, than his Doctors, or his Dogs.

SPARKISH
Pshaw, I know my interest, Sir, prethee hide me.

HORNER
Your Servant, Pinchwife,—what he knows us not—

MR PINCHWIFE

Come along.

[To his **WIFE** aside.

MRS PINCHWIFE
Pray, have you any Ballads, give me six-penny worth?

SPARKISH
We have no Ballads.

MRS PINCHWIFE
Then give me Covent-garden-Drollery, and a Play or two—Oh here's Tarugos Wiles, and the Slighted Maiden, I'll have them.

MR PINCHWIFE
No, Playes are not for your reading; come along, will you discover your self? [Apart to her.

HORNER
Who is that pretty Youth with him, Sparkish?

SPARKISH
I believe his Wife's Brother, because he's something like her, but I never saw her but once.

HORNER
Extreamly handsom, I have seen a face like it too; let us follow'em.

[Exeunt **MR PINCHWIFE, MRS PINCHWIFE, ALITHEA, LUCY, HORNER, DORILANT** following them.

HARCOURT
Come, Sparkish, your Mistriss saw you, and will be angry you go not to her; besides I wou'd fain be reconcil'd to her, which none but you can do, dear Friend.

SPARKISH
Well that's a better reason, dear Friend; I wou'd not go near her now, for her's, or my own sake, but I can deny you nothing; for though I have known thee a great while, never go, if I do not love thee, as well as a new Acquaintance.

HARCOURT
I am oblig'd to you indeed, dear Friend, I wou'd be well with her only, to be well with thee still; for these tyes to Wives usually dissolve all tyes to Friends: I wou'd be contented, she shou'd enjoy you a nights, but I wou'd have you to my self a dayes, as I have had, dear Friend.

SPARKISH
And thou shalt enjoy me a dayes, dear, dear Friend, never stir; and I'll be divorced from her, sooner than from thee; come along—

HARCOURT

So we are hard put to't, when we make our Rival our Procurer; but neither she, nor her Brother, wou'd let me come near her now: when all's done, a Rival is the best cloak to steal to a Mistress under, without suspicion; and when we have once got to her as we desire, we throw him off like other Cloaks.

[Aside.

[Exit **SPARKISH**, and **HARCOURT** following him.

[Re-enter **MR PINCHWIFE**, **MRS PINCHWIFE** in Man's Cloaths.

MR PINCHWIFE
Sister, if you will not go, we must leave you—[To **ALITHEA**]. The Fool her Gallant, and she, will muster up all the young santerers of this place, and they will leave their dear Seamstresses to follow us; what a swarm of Cuckolds, and Cuckold-makers are here? [Aside].
Come let's be gone Mistriss Margery.

MRS PINCHWIFE
Don't you believe that, I han't half my belly full of sights yet.

MR PINCHWIFE
Then walk this way.

MRS PINCHWIFE
Lord, what a power of brave signs are here! stay—the Bull's-head, the Rams-head, and the Stags-head, Dear—

MR PINCHWIFE
Nay, if every Husbands proper sign here were visible, they wou'd be all alike.

MRS PINCHWIFE
What d'ye mean by that, Bud?

MR PINCHWIFE
'Tis no matter—no matter, Bud.

MRS PINCHWIFE
Pray tell me; nay, I will know.

MR PINCHWIFE
They wou'd be all Bulls, Stags, and Rams heads.

[Exeunt **MR PINCHWIFE**, **MRS PINCHWIFE**.

[Re-enter **SPARKISH**, **HARCOURT**, **ALITHEA**, **LUCY**, at t'other door.

SPARKISH
Come, dear Madam, for my sake you shall be reconciled to him.

ALITHEA

For your sake I hate him.

HARCOURT

That's something too cruel, Madam, to hate me for his sake.

SPARKISH

Ay indeed, Madam, too, too cruel to me, to hate my Friend for my sake.

ALITHEA

I hate him because he is your Enemy; and you ought to hate him too, for making love to me, if you love me.

SPARKISH

That's a good one, I hate a Man for loving you; if he did love you, 'tis but what he can't help, and 'tis your fault not his, if he admires you: I hate a Man for being of my opinion, I'll ne'er do't, by the World.

ALITHEA

Is it for your honour or mine, to suffer a Man to make love to me, who am to marry you to morrow?

SPARKISH

Is it for your honour or mine, to have me jealous? That he makes love to you, is a sign you are handsome; and that I am not jealous, is a sign you are virtuous, that I think is for your honour.

ALITHEA

But 'tis your honour too, I am concerned for.

HARCOURT

But why, dearest Madam, will you be more concern'd for his honour, than he is himself; let his honour alone for my sake, and his, he, he, has no honour—

SPARKISH

How's that?

HARCOURT

But what, my dear Friend can guard himself.

SPARKISH

O ho—that's right again.

HARCOURT

Your care of his honour argues his neglect of it, which is no honour to my dear Friend here; therefore once more, let his honour go which way it will, dear Madam.

SPARKISH

Ay, ay, were it for my honour to marry a Woman, whose virtue I suspected, and cou'd not trust her in a Friends hands?

ALITHEA
Are you not afraid to loose me?

HARCOURT
He afraid to loose you, Madam! No, no—you may see how the most estimable, and most glorious Creature in the World, is valued by him; will you not see it?

SPARKISH
Right, honest Franck, I have that noble value for her, that I cannot be jealous of her.

ALITHEA
You mistake him, he means you care not for me, nor who has me.

SPARKISH
Lord, Madam, I see you are jealous; will you wrest a poor Mans meaning from his words?

ALITHEA
You astonish me, Sir, with your want of jealousie.

SPARKISH
And you make me guiddy, Madam, with your jealousie, and fears, and virtue, and honour; gad, I see virtue makes a Woman as troublesome, as a little reading, or learning.

ALITHEA
Monstrous!

LUCY
Well to see what easie Husbands these Women of quality can meet with, a poor Chamber-maid can never have such Lady-like luck; besides he's thrown away upon her, she'l make no use of her fortune, her blessing, none to a Gentleman, for a pure Cuckold, for it requires good breeding to be a Cuckold. [Behind].

ALITHEA
I tell you then plainly, he pursues me to marry me.

SPARKISH
Pshaw—

HARCOURT
Come, Madam, you see you strive in vain to make him jealous of me; my dear Friend is the kindest Creature in the World to me.

SPARKISH
Poor fellow.

HARCOURT

But his kindness only is not enough for me, without your favour; your good opinion, dear Madam, 'tis that must perfect my happiness: good Gentleman he believes all I say, wou'd you wou'd do so, jealous of me! I wou'd not wrong him nor you for the World.

SPARKISH
Look you there; hear him, hear him, and do not walk away so.

ALITHEA walks carelessly, to and fro.

HARCOURT
I love you, Madam, so—

SPARKISH
How's that! Nay—now you begin to go too far indeed.

HARCOURT
So much I confess, I say I love you, that I wou'd not have you miserable, and cast your self away upon so unworthy, and inconsiderable a thing, as what you see here,

Clapping his hand on his breast, points at **SPARKISH**.

SPARKISH
No faith, I believe thou woud'st not, now his meaning is plain: but I knew before thou woud'st not wrong me nor her.

HARCOURT
No, no, Heavens forbid, the glory of her Sex shou'd fall so, low as into the embraces of such a contemptible Wretch, the last of Mankind—my dear Friend here—I injure him.

[Embracing **SPARKISH**.

ALITHEA
Very well.

SPARKISH
No, no, dear Friend, I knew it Madam, you see he will rather wrong himself than me, in giving himself such names.

ALITHEA
Do not you understand him yet?

SPARKISH
Yes, how modestly he speaks of himself, poor Fellow.

ALITHEA
Methinks he speaks impudently of your self, since— before your self too, insomuch that I can no longer suffer his scurrilous abusiveness to you, no more than his love to me.

[*Offers to go.*

SPARKISH
Nay, nay, Madam, pray stay, his love to you: Lord, Madam, has he not spoke yet plain enough?

ALITHEA
Yes indeed, I shou'd think so.

SPARKISH
Well then, by the World, a Man can't speak civilly to a Woman now, but presently she says, he makes love to her: Nay, Madam, you shall stay, with your pardon, since you have not yet understood him, till he has made an eclaircisment of his love to you, that is what kind of love it is; answer to thy Catechisme: Friend, do you love my Mistriss here?

HARCOURT
Yes, I wish she wou'd not doubt it.

SPARKISH
But how do you love her?

HARCOURT
With all my Soul.

ALITHEA
I thank him, methinks he speaks plain enough now.

SPARKISH
You are out still. [to **ALITHEA**].
But with what kind of love, Harcourt?

HARCOURT
With the best, and truest love in the World.

SPARKISH
Look you there then, that is with no matrimonial love, I'm sure.

ALITHEA
How's that, do you say matrimonial love is not best?

SPARKISH
Gad, I went too far e're I was aware: But speak for thy self Harcourt, you said you wou'd not wrong me, nor her.

HARCOURT
No, no, Madam, e'n take him for Heaven's sake.

SPARKISH
Look you there, Madam.

HARCOURT
Who shou'd in all justice be yours, he that loves you most.

[Claps his hand on his breast.

ALITHEA
Look you there, Mr. Sparkish, who's that?

SPARKISH
Who shou'd it be? go on Harcourt.

HARCOURT
Who loves you more than Women, Titles, or fortune Fools.

[Points at **SPARKISH**.

SPARKISH
Look you there, he means me stil, for he points at me.

ALITHEA
Ridiculous!

HARCOURT
Who can only match your Faith, and constancy in love.

SPARKISH
Ay.

HARCOURT
Who knows, if it be possible, how to value so much beauty and virtue.

SPARKISH
Ay.

HARCOURT
Whose love can no more be equall'd in the world, than that Heavenly form of yours.

SPARKISH
No—

HARCOURT
Who cou'd no more suffer a Rival, than your absence, and yet cou'd no more suspect your virtue, than his own constancy in his love to you.

SPARKISH
No—

HARCOURT
Who in fine loves you better than his eyes, that first made him love you.

SPARKISH
Ay—nay, Madam, faith you shan't go, till—

ALITHEA
Have a care, lest you make me stay too long—

SPARKISH
But till he has saluted you; that I may be assur'd you are friends, after his honest advice and declaration: Come pray, Madam, be friends with him.

[Enter **MR PINCHWIFE, MRS PINCHWIFE.**

ALITHEA
You must pardon me, Sir, that I am not yet so obedient to you.

MR PINCHWIFE
What, invite your Wife to kiss Men? Monstrous, are you not asham'd? I will never forgive you.

SPARKISH
Are you not asham'd, that I shou'd have more confidence in the chastity of your Family, than you have; you must not teach me, I am a man of honour, Sir, though I am frank and free; I am frank, Sir—

MR PINCHWIFE
Very frank, Sir, to share your Wife with your friends.

SPARKISH
He is an humble, menial Friend, such as reconciles the differences of the Marriage-bed; you know Man and Wife do not alwayes agree, I design him for that use, therefore wou'd have him well with my Wife.

MR PINCHWIFE
A menial Friend—you will get a great many menial Friends, by shewing your Wife as you do.

SPARKISH
What then, it may be I have a pleasure in't, as I have to shew fine Clothes, at a Play-house the first day, and count money before poor Rogues.

MR PINCHWIFE
He that shews his wife, or money will be in danger of having them borrowed sometimes.

SPARKISH
I love to be envy'd, and wou'd not marry a Wife, that I alone cou'd love; loving alone is as dull, as eating alone; is it not a frank age, and I am a frank Person? and to tell you the truth, it may be I love to have Rivals in a Wife, they make her seem to a Man still, but as a kept Mistriss; and so good night, for I must to Whitehal. Madam, I hope you are now reconcil'd to my Friend; and so I wish you a good night,

Madam, and sleep if you can, for to morrow you know I must visit you early with a Canonical Gentleman. Good night dear Harcourt.

[Exit **SPARKISH**.

HARCOURT
Madam, I hope you will not refuse my visit to morrow, if it shou'd be earlyer, with a Canonical Gentleman, than Mr. Sparkish's.

MR PINCHWIFE
This Gentle-woman is yet under my care, therefore you must yet forbear your freedom with her, Sir.

[Coming between **ALITHEA** and **HARCOURT**.

HARCOURT
Must, Sir—

MR PINCHWIFE
Yes, Sir, she is my Sister.

HARCOURT
'Tis well she is, Sir—for I must be her Servant, Sir. Madam—

MR PINCHWIFE
Come away Sister, we had been gone, if it had not been for you, and so avoided these lewd Rakehells, who seem to haunt us.

[Enter **HORNER, DORILANT** to them.

HORNER
How now Pinchwife?

MR PINCHWIFE
Your Servant.

HORNER
What, I see a little time in the Country makes a Man turn wild and unsociable, and only fit to converse with his Horses, Dogs, and his Herds.

MR PINCHWIFE
I have business, Sir, and must mind it; your business is pleasure, therefore you and I must go different wayes.

HORNER
Well, you may go on, but this pretty young Gentleman—

[Takes hold of **MRS PINCHWIFE**.

HARCOURT
The Lady—

DORILANT
And the Maid—

HORNER
Shall stay with us, for I suppose their business is the same with ours, pleasure.

MR PINCHWIFE
'Sdeath he knows her, she carries it so sillily, yet if he does not, I shou'd be more silly to discover it first.
[Aside].

ALITHEA
Pray, let us go, Sir.

MR PINCHWIFE
Come, come—

HORNER
Had you not rather stay with us? [to **MRS PINCHWIFE**] Prethee Pinchwife, who is this pretty young
Gentleman?

MR PINCHWIFE
One to whom I'm a guardian. [Aside]. I wish I cou'd keep her out of your hands—

HORNER
Who is he? I never saw any thing so pretty in all my life.

MR PINCHWIFE
Pshaw, do not look upon him so much, he's a poor bashful youth, you'l put him out of countenance.
Come away Brother.

[Offers to take her away.

HORNER
O your Brother!

MR PINCHWIFE
Yes, my Wifes Brother; come, come, she'l stay supper for us.

HORNER
I thought so, for he is very like her I saw you at the Play with, whom I told you, I was in love with.

MRS PINCHWIFE
O Jeminy! is this he that was in love with me, I am glad on't I vow, for he's a curious fine Gentleman, and
I love him already too. [Aside]. Is this he Bud? [To **MR PINCHWIFE**.

MR PINCHWIFE

Come away, come away. [To his **WIFE**.

HORNER

Why, what hast are you in? why wont you let me talk with him?

MR PINCHWIFE

Because you'l debauch him, he's yet young and innocent, and I wou'd not have him debauch'd for any thing in the World. [Aside]. How she gazes on him! the Divel—

HORNER

Harcourt, Dorilant, look you here, this is the likeness of that Dowdey he told us of, his Wife, did you ever see a lovelyer Creature? the Rogue has reason to be jealous of his Wife, since she is like him, for she wou'd make all that see her, in love with her.

HARCOURT

And as I remember now, she is as like him here as can be.

DORILANT

She is indeed very pretty, if she be like him.

HORNER

Very pretty, a very pretty commendation—she is a glorious Creature, beautiful beyond all things I ever beheld.

MR PINCHWIFE

So, so.

HARCOURT

More beautiful than a Poets first Mistriss of Imagination.

HORNER

Or another Mans last Mistriss of flesh and blood.

MRS PINCHWIFE

Nay, now you jeer, Sir; pray don't jeer me—

MR PINCHWIFE

Come, come. [Aside]. By Heavens she'l discover her self.

HORNER

I speak of your Sister, Sir.

MR PINCHWIFE

Ay, but saying she was handsom, if like him, made him blush. [Aside]. I am upon a wrack—

HORNER

Methinks he is so handsom, he shou'd not be a Man.

MR PINCHWIFE

O there 'tis out, he has discovered her, I am not able to suffer any longer. [To his **WIFE**]. Come, come away, I say—

HORNER

Nay, by your leave, Sir, he shall not go yet— Harcourt, Dorilant, let us torment this jealous Rogue a little.

[To them.

HARCOURT, DORILANT

How?

HORNER

I'll shew you.

MR PINCHWIFE

Come, pray let him go, I cannot stay fooling any longer; I tell you his Sister stays supper for us.

HORNER

Do's she, come then we'l all go sup with her and thee.

MR PINCHWIFE

No, now I think on't, having staid so long for us, I warrant she's gone to bed—[Aside]. I wish she and I were well out of their hands— Come, I must rise early to morrow, come.

HORNER

Well then, if she be gone to bed, I wish her and you a good night. But pray, young Gentleman, present my humble service to her.

MRS PINCHWIFE

Thank you heartily, Sir.

MR PINCHWIFE

S'death, she will discover her self yet in spight of me. [Aside]. He is something more civil to you, for your kindness to his Sister, than I am, it seems.

HORNER

Tell her, dear sweet little Gentleman, for all your Brother there, that you have reviv'd the love, I had for her at first sight in the Play-house.

MRS PINCHWIFE

But did you love her indeed, and indeed?

MR PINCHWIFE

So, so. [Aside] Away, I say.

HORNER

Nay stay; yes indeed, and indeed, pray do you tell her so, and give her this kiss from me.

[Kisses her.

MR PINCHWIFE
O Heavens! what do I suffer; now 'tis too plain he knows her, and yet—[Aside.

HORNER
And this, and this—

[Kisses her again.

MRS PINCHWIFE
What do you kiss me for, I am no Woman.

MR PINCHWIFE
So—there 'tis out. [Aside]. Come, I cannot, nor will stay any longer.

HORNER
Nay, they shall send your Lady a kiss too; here Harcourt, Dorilant, will you not?

[They kiss her.

MR PINCHWIFE
How, do I suffer this? was I not accusing another just now, for this rascally, patience, in permitting his Wife to be kiss'd before his face? ten thousand ulcers gnaw away their lips. [Aside]. Come, come.

HORNER
Good night dear little Gentleman; Madam goodnight; farewel Pinchwife. [Apart to **HARCOURT** and **DORILANT**] Did not I tell you, I wou'd raise his jealous gall.

[Exeunt **HORNER, HARCOURT,** and **DORILANT**.

MR PINCHWIFE
So they are gone at last; stay, let me see first if the Coach be at this door.

[Exit.

HORNER
What not gone yet? will you be sure to do as I desired you, sweet Sir?

HORNER, HARCOURT, DORILANT return.

MRS PINCHWIFE
Sweet Sir, but what will you give me then?

HORNER
Any thing, come away into the next walk.

[Exit **HORNER**, haling away **MRS PINCHWIFE**.

ALITHEA
Hold, hold,—what d'ye do?

LUCY
Stay, stay, hold—

HARCOURT
Hold Madam, hold, let him present him, he'l come presently; nay, I will never let you go, till you answer my question.

ALITHEA, LUCY strugling with **HARCOURT**, and **DORILANT**.

LUCY
For God's sake, Sir, I must follow'em.

DORILANT
No, I have something to present you with too, you shan't follow them.

MR PINCHWIFE returns.

MR PINCHWIFE
Where?—how?—what's become of? gone— whither?

LUCY
He's only gone with the Gentleman, who will give him something, an't please your Worship.

MR PINCHWIFE
Something—give him something, with a Pox— where are they?

ALITHEA
In the next walk only, Brother.

MR PINCHWIFE
Only, only; where, where?

[Exit **MR PINCHWIFE**, and returns presently, then goes out again.

HARCOURT
What's the matter with him? why so much concern'd? but dearest Madam—

ALITHEA
Pray, let me go, Sir, I have said, and suffer'd enough already.

HARCOURT
Then you will not look upon, nor pitty my sufferings?

ALITHEA

To look upon'em, when I cannot help'em, were cruelty, not pitty, therefore I will never see you more.

HARCOURT

Let me then, Madam, have my priviledge of a banished Lover, complaining or railing, and giving you but a farewell reason; why, if you cannot condescend to marry me, you shou'd not take that wretch my Rival.

ALITHEA

He only, not you, since my honour is engag'd so far to him, can give me a reason, why I shou'd not marry him; but if he be true, and what I think him to me, I must be so to him; your Servant, Sir.

HARCOURT

Have Women only constancy when 'tis a vice, and like fortune only true to fools?

DORILANT

Thou sha't not stir thou robust Creature, you see I can deal with you, thereforefore you shou'd stay the rather, and be kind. [To **LUCY**, who struggles to get from him].

[Enter **MR PINCHWIFE**.

MR PINCHWIFE

Gone, gone, not to be found; quite gone, ten thousand plagues go with'em; which way went they?

ALITHEA

But into t'other walk, Brother.

LUCY

Their business will be done presently sure, an't please your Worship, it can't be long in doing I'm sure on't.

ALITHEA

Are they not there?

MR PINCHWIFE

No, you know where they are, you infamous Wretch, Eternal shame of your Family, which you do not dishonour enough your self, you think, but you must help her to do it too, thou legion of Bawds.

ALITHEA

Good Brother.

MR PINCHWIFE

Damn'd, damn'd Sister.

ALITHEA

Look you here, she's coming.

[Enter **MRS PINCHWIFE** in Mans cloaths, running with her hat under her arm, full of Oranges and dried fruit, **HORNER** following.

MRS PINCHWIFE
O dear Bud, look you here what I have got, see.

MR PINCHWIFE
And what I have got here too, which you can't see.

[Aside rubbing his forehead.

MRS PINCHWIFE
The fine Gentleman has given me better things yet.

MR PINCHWIFE
Ha's he so? [Aside]. Out of breath and colour'd— I must hold yet.

HORNER
I have only given your little Brother an Orange, Sir.

MR PINCHWIFE
Thank you, Sir. [To **HORNER**]. You have only squeez'd my Orange, I suppose, and given it me again; yet I must have a City-patience. [Aside]. Come, come away—[To his **WIFE**.

MRS PINCHWIFE
Stay, till I have put up my fine things, Bud.

[Enter **SIR JASPAR FIDGET**.

SIR JASPAR
O Master Horner, come, come, the Ladies stay for you; your Mistriss, my Wife, wonders you make not more hast to her.

HORNER
I have staid this halfhour for you here, and 'tis your fault I am not now with your Wife.

SIR JASPAR
But pray, don't let her know so much, the truth on't is, I was advancing a certain Project to his Majesty, about—I'll tell you.

HORNER
No, let's go, and hear it at your house: Good night sweet little Gentleman; one kiss more, you'l remember me now I hope.

[Kisses her.

DORILANT

What, Sir Jaspar, will you separate Friends? he promis'd to sup with us; and if you take him to your house, you'l be in danger of our company too.

SIR JASPAR
Alas Gentlemen my house is not fit for you, there are none but civil Women there, which are not for your turn; he you know can bear with the society of civil Women, now, ha, ha, ha; besides he's one of my Family;—he's— heh, heh, heh.

DORILANT
What is he?

SIR JASPAR
Faith my Eunuch, since you'l have it, heh, he, he.

[Exit **SIR JASPAR FIDGET** and **HORNER**.

DORILANT
I rather wish thou wert his, or my Cuckold: Harcourt, what a good Cuckold is lost there, for want of a Man to make him one; thee and I cannot have Horners privilege, who can make use of it.

HARCOURT
Ay, to poor Horner 'tis like coming to an estate at threescore, when a Man can't be the better for't.

MR PINCHWIFE
Come.

MRS PINCHWIFE
Presently Bud.

DORILANT
Come let us go too: Madam, your Servant. [To **ALITHEA**
Good night Strapper.—

[To **LUCY**

HARCOURT
Madam, though you will not let me have a good day, or night, I wish you one; but dare not name the other half of my wish.

ALITHEA
Good night, Sir, for ever.

MRS PINCHWIFE
I don't know where to put this here, dear Bud, you shall eat it; nay, you shall have part of the fine Gentlemans good things, or treat as you call it, when we come home.

MR PINCHWIFE
Indeed I deserve it, since I furnish'd the best part of it.

[Strikes away the Orange.

The Gallant treats, presents, and gives the Ball;
But 'tis the absent Cuckold, pays for all.

ACT IV

SCENE I

IN PINCHWIFE'S HOUSE IN THE MORNING

LUCY, ALITHEA dress'd in new Cloths.

LUCY
Well—Madam, now have I dress'd you, and set you out with so many ornaments, and spent upon you ounces of essence, and pulvilio; and all this for no other purpose, but as People adorn, and perfume a Corps, for a stinking second-hand-grave, such or as bad I think Master Sparkish's bed.

ALITHEA
Hold your peace.

LUCY
Nay, Madam, I will ask you the reason, why you wou'd banish poor Master Harcourt for ever from your sight? how cou'd you be so hard-hearted?

ALITHEA
'Twas because I was not hard-hearted.

LUCY
No, no; 'twas 'stark love and kindness, I warrant.

ALITHEA
It was so; I wou'd see him no more, because I love him.

LUCY
Hey day, a very pretty reason.

ALITHEA
You do not understand me.

LUCY
I wish you may your self.

ALITHEA
I was engag'd to marry, you see, another man, whom my justice will not suffer me to deceive, or injure.

LUCY

Can there be a greater cheat, or wrong done to a Man, than to give him your person, without your heart, I shou'd make a conscience of it.

ALITHEA

I'll retrieve it for him after I am married a while.

LUCY

The Woman that marries to love better, will be as much mistaken, as the Wencher that marries to live better. No, Madam, marrying to encrease love, is like gaming to become rich; alas you only loose, what little stock you had before.

ALITHEA

I find by your Rhetorick you have been brib'd to betray me.

LUCY

Only by his merit, that has brib'd your heart you see against your word, and rigid honour; but what a Divel is this honour? 'tis sure a disease in the head, like the Megrim, or Falling-sickness, that alwayes hurries People away to do themselves mischief; Men loose their lives by it: Women what's dearer to'em, their love, the life of life.

ALITHEA

Come, pray talk you no more of honour, nor Master Harcourt; I wish the other wou'd come, to secure my fidelity to him, and his right in me.

LUCY

You will marry him then?

ALITHEA

Certainly, I have given him already my word, and will my hand too, to make it good when he comes.

LUCY

Well, I wish I may never stick pin more, if he be not an errant Natural, to t'other fine Gentleman.

ALITHEA

I own he wants the wit of Harcourt, which I will dispense withal, for another want he has, which is want of jealousie, which men of wit seldom want.

LUCY

Lord, Madam, what shou'd you do with a fool to your Husband, you intend to be honest don't you? then that husbandly virtue, credulity, is thrown away upon you.

ALITHEA

He only that could suspect my virtue, shou'd have cause to do it; 'tis Sparkish's confidence in my truth, that obliges me to be so faithful to him.

LUCY

You are not sure his opinion may last.

ALITHEA
I am satisfied, 'tis impossible for him to be jealous, after the proofs I have had of him: Jealousie in a Husband, Heaven defend me from it, it begets a thousand plagues to a poor Woman, the loss of her honour, her quiet, and her—

LUCY
And her pleasure.

ALITHEA
What d'ye mean, Impertinent?

LUCY
Liberty is a great pleasure, Madam.

ALITHEA
I say loss of her honour, her quiet, nay, her life sometimes; and what's as bad almost, the loss of this Town, that is, she is sent into the Country, which is the last ill usage of a Husband to a Wife, I think.

LUCY
O do's the wind lye there? [Aside]. Then of necessity, Madam, you think a man must carry his Wife into the Country, if he be wise; the Country is as terrible I find to our young English Ladies, as a Monastery to those abroad: and on my Virginity, I think they wou'd rather marry a London-Goaler, than a high Sheriff of a County, since neither can stir from his employment: formerly Women of wit married Fools, for a great Estate, a fine seat, or the like; but now 'tis for a pretty seat only in Lincoln's Inn-fields, St. James's-fields, or the Pall-mall.

[Enter to them **SPARKISH**, and **HARCOURT** dress'd like a Parson.

SPARKISH
Madam, your humble Servant, a happy day to you, and to us all.

HARCOURT
Amen.—

ALITHEA
Who have we here?

SPARKISH
My Chaplain faith—O Madam, poor Harcourt remembers his humble service to you; and in obedience to your last commands, refrains coming into your sight.

ALITHEA
Is not that he?

SPARKISH

No, fye no; but to shew that he ne're intended to hinder our Match has sent his Brother here to joyn our hands: when I get me a Wife, I must get her a Chaplain, according to the Custom; this is his Brother, and my Chaplain.

ALITHEA
His Brother?

LUCY
And your Chaplain, to preach in your Pulpit then—[Aside.

ALITHEA
His Brother!

SPARKISH
Nay, I knew you wou'd not believe it; I told you, Sir, she wou'd take you for your Brother Frank.

ALITHEA
Believe it!

LUCY
His Brother! hah, ha, he, he has a trick left still it seems—[Aside.

SPARKISH
Come my dearest, pray let us go to Church before the Canonical hour is past.

ALITHEA
For shame you are abus'd still.

SPARKISH
By the World 'tis strange now you are so incredulous.

ALITHEA
'Tis strange you are so credulous.

SPARKISH
Dearest of my life, hear me, I tell you this is Ned Harcourt of Cambridge, by the world, you see he has a sneaking Colledg look; 'tis true he's something like his Brother Frank and they differ from each other no more than in their age, for they were Twins.

LUCY
Hah, ha, he.

ALITHEA
Your Servant, Sir, I cannot be so deceiv'd, though you are; but come let's hear, how do you know what you affirm so confidently?

SPARKISH

Why, I'll tell you all; Frank Harcourt coming to me this morning, to wish me joy and present his service to you: I ask'd him, if he cou'd help me to a Parson; whereupon he told me, he had a Brother in Town who was in Orders, and he went straight away, and sent him, you see there, to me.

ALITHEA
Yes, Frank goes, and puts on a black-coat, then tell's you, he is Ned, that's all you have for't.

SPARKISH
Pshaw, pshaw, I tell you by the same token, the Midwife put her Garter about Frank's neck, to know'em asunder, they were so like.

ALITHEA
Frank tell's you this too.

SPARKISH
Ay, and Ned there too; nay, they are both in a Story.

ALITHEA
So, so, very foolish.

SPARKISH
Lord, if you won't believe one, you had best trye him by your Chamber-maid there; for Chamber-maids must needs know Chaplains from other Men, they are so us'd to'em.

LUCY
Let's see; nay, I'll be sworn he has the Canonical smirk, and the filthy, clammy palm of a Chaplain.

ALITHEA
Well, most reverend Doctor, pray let us make an end of this fooling.

HARCOURT
With all my soul, Divine, Heavenly Creature, when you please.

ALITHEA
He speaks like a Chaplain indeed.

SPARKISH
Why, was there not, soul, Divine, Heavenly, in what he said.

ALITHEA
Once more, most impertinent Black-coat, cease your persecution, and let us have a Conclusion of this ridiculous love.

HARCOURT
I had forgot, I must sute my Stile to my Coat, or I wear it in vain. [Aside].

ALITHEA
I have no more patience left, let us make once an end of this troublesome Love, I say.

HARCOURT

So be it, Seraphick Lady, when your Honour shall think it meet, and convenient so to do.

SPARKISH

Gad I'm sure none but a Chaplain cou'd speak so, I think.

ALITHEA

Let me tell you Sir, this dull trick will not serve your turn, though you delay our marriage, you shall not hinder it.

HARCOURT

Far be it from me, Munificent Patroness, to delay your Marriage, I desire nothing more than to marry you presently, which I might do, if you your self wou'd; for my Noble, Good-natur'd and thrice Generous Patron here wou'd not hinder it.

SPARKISH

No, poor man, not I faith.

HARCOURT

And now, Madam, let me tell you plainly, no body else shall marry you by Heavens, I'll die first, for I'm sure I shou'd die after it.

LUCY

How his Love has made him forget his Function, as I have seen it in real Parsons.

ALITHEA

That was spoken like a Chaplain too, now you understand him, I hope.

SPARKISH

Poor man, he takes it hainously to be refus'd; I can't blame him, 'tis putting an indignity upon him not to be suffer'd, but you'l pardon me Madam, it shan't be, he shall marry us, come away, pray Madam.

LUCY

Hah, ha, he, more ado! 'tis late.

ALITHEA

Invincible stupidity, I tell you he wou'd marry me, as your Rival, not as your Chaplain.

SPARKISH

Come, come Madam.

[Pulling her away.

LUCY

I pray Madam, do not refuse this Reverend Divine, the honour and satisfaction of marrying you; for I dare say, he has set his heart upon't, good Doctor.

ALITHEA
What can you hope, or design by this?

HARCOURT
I cou'd answer her, a reprieve for a day only, often revokes a hasty doom; at worst, if she will not take mercy on me, and let me marry her, I have at least the Lovers second pleasure, hindring my Rivals enjoyment, though but for a time.

SPARKISH
Come Madam, 'tis e'ne twelve a clock, and my Mother charg'd me never to be married out of the Canonical hours; come, come, Lord here's such a deal of modesty, I warrant the first day.

LUCY
Yes, an't please your Worship, married women shew all their Modesty the first day, because married men shew all their love the first day.

[Exeunt **SPARKISH, ALITHEA, HARCOURT**, and **LUCY**

THE SCENE CHANGES TO A BED-CHAMBER

Where appear **MR PINCHWIFE** and **MRS PINCHWIFE**.

MR PINCHWIFE
Come tell me, I say.

MRS PINCHWIFE
Lord, han't I told it an hundred times over.

MR PINCHWIFE
I wou'd try, if in the repetition of the ungrateful tale, I cou'd find her altering it in the least circumstance, for if her story be false, she is so too. [Aside]. Come how was't Baggage?

MRS PINCHWIFE
Lord, what pleasure you take to hear it sure!

MR PINCHWIFE
No, you take more in telling it I find, but speak how was't?

MRS PINCHWIFE
He carried me up into the house, next to the Exchange.

MR PINCHWIFE
So, and you two were only in the room.

MRS PINCHWIFE
Yes, for he sent away a youth that was there, for some dryed fruit, and China Oranges.

MR PINCHWIFE

Did he so? Damn him for it—and for—

MRS PINCHWIFE

But presently came up the Gentlewoman of the house.

MR PINCHWIFE

O 'twas well she did, but what did he do whilest the fruit came?

MRS PINCHWIFE

He kiss'd me an hundred times, and told me he fancied he kiss'd my fine Sister, meaning me you know, whom he said he lov'd with all his Soul, and bid me be sure to tell her so, and to desire her to be at her window, by eleven of the clock this morning, and he wou'd walk under it at that time.

MR PINCHWIFE

And he was as good as his word, very punctual, a pox reward him for't. [Aside].

MRS PINCHWIFE

Well, and he said if you were not within, he wou'd come up to her, meaning me you know, Bud, still.

MR PINCHWIFE

So—he knew her certainly, but for this confession, I am oblig'd to her simplicity. [Aside]. But what you stood very still, when he kiss'd you?

MRS PINCHWIFE

Yes I warrant you, wou'd you have had me discover'd my self?

MR PINCHWIFE

But you told me, he did some beastliness to you, as you call'd it, what was't?

MRS PINCHWIFE

Why, he put—

MR PINCHWIFE

What?

MRS PINCHWIFE

Why he put the tip of his tongue between my lips, and so musl'd me—and I said, I'd bite it.

MR PINCHWIFE

An eternal canker seize it, for a dog.

MRS PINCHWIFE

Nay, you need not be so angry with him neither, for to say truth, he has the sweetest breath I ever knew.

MR PINCHWIFE

The Devil—you were satisfied with it then, and wou'd do it again.

MRS PINCHWIFE
Not unless he shou'd force me.

MR PINCHWIFE
Force you, changeling! I tell you no woman can be forced.

MRS PINCHWIFE
Yes, but she may sure, by such a one as he, for he's a proper, goodly strong man, 'tis hard, let me tell you, to resist him.

MR PINCHWIFE
So, 'tis plain she loves him, yet she has not love enough to make her conceal it from me, but the sight of him will increase her aversion for me, and love for him; and that love instruct her how to deceive me, and satisfie him, all Ideot as she is: Love, 'twas he gave women first their craft, their art of deluding; out of natures hands, they came plain, open, silly and fit for slaves, as she and Heaven intended'em; but damn'd Love—Well—I must strangle that little Monster, whilest I can deal with him. Go fetch Pen, Ink and Paper out of the next room:

MRS PINCHWIFE
Yes Bud.

[Exit **MRS PINCHWIFE**.

MR PINCHWIFE
Why should Women have more invention in love than men? It can only be, because they have more desires, more solliciting passions, more lust, and more of the Devil.

[**MRS PINCHWIFE** returns.

Come, Minks, sit down and write.

MRS PINCHWIFE
Ay, dear Bud, but I can't do't very well.

MR PINCHWIFE
I wish you cou'd not at all.

MRS PINCHWIFE
But what shou'd I write for?

MR PINCHWIFE
I'll have you write a Letter to your Lover.

MRS PINCHWIFE
O Lord, to the fine Gentleman a Letter!

MR PINCHWIFE
Yes, to the fine Gentleman.

MRS PINCHWIFE
Lord, you do but jeer; sure you jest.

MR PINCHWIFE
I am not so merry, come write as I bid you.

MRS PINCHWIFE
What, do you think I am a fool?

MR PINCHWIFE
She's afraid I would not dictate any love to him, therefore she's unwilling; but you had best begin.

MRS PINCHWIFE
Indeed, and indeed, but I won't, so I won't.

MR PINCHWIFE
Why?

MRS PINCHWIFE
Because he's in Town, you may send for him if you will.

MR PINCHWIFE
Very well, you wou'd have him brought to you; is it come to this? I say take the pen and write, or you'll provoke me.

MRS PINCHWIFE
Lord, what d'ye make a fool of me for? Don't I know that Letters are never writ, but from the Countrey to London, and from London into the Countrey; now he's in Town, and I am in Town too; therefore I can't write to him you know.

MR PINCHWIFE
So I am glad it is no worse, she is innocent enough yet—[Aside]. Yes you may when your Husband bids you write Letters to people that are in Town.

MRS PINCHWIFE
O may I so! Then I'm satisfied.

MR PINCHWIFE
Come begin—Sir—

[Dictates.

MRS PINCHWIFE
Shan't I say, Dear Sir? You know one says always something more than bare Sir.

MR PINCHWIFE
Write as I bid you, or I will write Whore with this Penknife in your Face.

MRS PINCHWIFE
Nay good Bud—Sir—

[She writes.

MR PINCHWIFE
Though I suffer'd last night your nauseous, loath'd Kisses and Embraces—Write

MRS PINCHWIFE
Nay, why shou'd I say so, you know I told you, he had a sweet breath.

MR PINCHWIFE
Write.

MRS PINCHWIFE
Let me but put out, loath'd.

MR PINCHWIFE
Write I say.

MRS PINCHWIFE
Well then.

[Writes.

MR PINCHWIFE
Let's see what have you writ?
Though I suffer'd last night your kisses and embraces—

[Takes the paper, and reads.

Thou impudent creature, where is nauseous and loath'd?

MRS PINCHWIFE
I can't abide to write such filthy words.

MR PINCHWIFE
Once more write as I'd have you, and question it not, or I will spoil thy writing with this, I will stab out those eyes that cause my mischief.

[Holds up the penknife.

MRS PINCHWIFE
O Lord, I will.

MR PINCHWIFE
So—so—Let's see now!

[Reads.
Though I suffer'd last night your nauseous, loath'd kisses, and embraces; Go on—Yet I would not have you presume that you shall ever repeat them—So—

[She writes.

MRS PINCHWIFE
I have writ it.

MR PINCHWIFE
On then—I then conceal'd my self from your knowledge, to avoid your insolencies—

[She writes.

MRS PINCHWIFE
So—

MR PINCHWIFE
The same reason now I am out of your hands—

[She writes.

MRS PINCHWIFE
So—

MR PINCHWIFE
Makes me own to you my unfortunate, though innocent frolick, of being in man's cloths.

[She writes.

MRS PINCHWIFE
So—

MR PINCHWIFE
That you may for ever more cease to pursue her, who hates and detests you—

[She writes on.

MRS PINCHWIFE
So—h—

[Sighs.

MR PINCHWIFE
What do you sigh?—detests you—as much as she loves her Husband and her Honour—

MRS PINCHWIFE

I vow Husband he'll ne'er believe, I shou'd write such a Letter.

MR PINCHWIFE

What he'd expect a kinder from you? come now your name only.

MRS PINCHWIFE

What, shan't I say your most faithful, humble Servant till death?

MR PINCHWIFE

No, tormenting Fiend; her stile I find wou'd be very soft. [Aside]. Come wrap it up now, whilest I go fetch wax and a candle; and write on the back side, for Mr. Horner.

[Exit **MR PINCHWIFE**.

MRS PINCHWIFE

For Mr. Horner—So, I am glad he has told me his name; Dear Mr. Horner, but why should I send thee such a Letter, that will vex thee, and make thee angry with me;—well I will not send it—Ay but then my husband will kill me—for I see plainly, he won't let me love Mr. Horner—but what care I for my Husband—I won't so I won't send poor Mr. Horner such a Letter—but then my Husband—But oh—what if I writ at bottom, my Husband made me write it—Ay but then my Husband wou'd see't—Can one have no shift, ah, a London woman wou'd have had a hundred presently; stay—what if I shou'd write a Letter, and wrap it up like this, and write upon't too; ay but then my Husband wou'd see't—I don't know what to do—But yet y vads I'll try, so I will— for I will not send this Letter to poor Mr. Horner, come what will on't.

Dear, Sweet Mr. Horner—So— my Husband wou'd have me send you a base, rude, unmannerly Letter—but

[She writes, and repeats what she hath writ.

I won't—so—and wou'd have me forbid you loving me—but I wont—so—and wou'd have me say to you, I hate you poor Mr. Horner—but I won't tell a lye for him—there—for I'm sure if you and I were in the Countrey at cards together,—so—I cou'd not help treading on your Toe under the Table—so—or rubbing knees with you, and staring in your face, 'till you saw me —very well—and then looking down, and blushing for an hour together—so—but I must make haste before my Husband come; and now he has taught me to write Letters: You shall have longer ones from me, who am

Dear, dear, poor dear Mr. Horner, your most Humble Friend, and Servant to command 'till death, Margery Pinchwife.

Stay I must give him a hint at bottom—so—now wrap it up just like t'other—so—now write for Mr. Horner,— But oh now what shall I do with it? for here comes my Husband.

[Enter **MR PINCHWIFE**.

MR PINCHWIFE

I have been detained by a Sparkish Coxcomb, who pretended a visit to me; but I fear 'twas to my Wife. [Aside]. What, have you done?

MRS PINCHWIFE
Ay, ay Bud, just now.

MR PINCHWIFE
Let's see't, what d'ye tremble for; what, you wou'd not have it go?

MRS PINCHWIFE
Here—No I must not give him that, so I had been served if I

[He opens, and reads the first Letter.

—had given him this. [Aside].

MR PINCHWIFE
Come, where's the Wax and Seal?

MRS PINCHWIFE
Lord, what shall I do now? Nay then I have it—[Aside].
Pray let me see't, Lord you think—

[Snatches the Letter from him, changes it for the other, seals it, and delivers it to him.

—me so errand a fool, I cannot seal a Letter, I will do't, so I will.

MR PINCHWIFE
Nay, I believe you will learn that, and other things too, which I wou'd not have you.

MRS PINCHWIFE
So, han't I done it curiously?
I think I have, there's my Letter going to Mr. Horner; since he'll needs have me send Letters to Folks. [Aside.

MR PINCHWIFE
'Tis very well, but I warrant, you wou'd not have it go now?

MRS PINCHWIFE
Yes indeed, but I wou'd, Bud, now.

MR PINCHWIFE
Well you are a good Girl then, come let me lock you up in your chamber, 'till I come back; and be sure you come not within three strides of the window, when I am gone; for I have a spye in the street.

[Exit **MRS PINCHWIFE**

At least, 'tis fit she think so, if we do

[**MR PINCHWIFE** locks the door.

—not cheat women, they'll cheat us; and fraud may be justly used with secret enemies, of which a Wife is the most dangerous; and he that has a handsome one to keep, and a Frontier Town, must provide against treachery, rather than open Force—Now I have secur'd all within, I'll deal with the Foe without with false intelligence.

[Holds up the Letter.

[Exit **MR PINCHWIFE**.

THE SCENE CHANGE'S TO HORNER'S LODGING.

QUACK and **HORNER**.

QUACK
Well Sir, how fadges the new design; have you not the luck of all your brother Projectors, to deceive only your self at last.

HORNER
No, good Domine Doctor, I deceive you it seems, and others too; for the grave Matrons, and old ridgid Husbands think me as unfit for love, as they are; but their Wives, Sisters and Daughters, know some of'em better things already.

QUACK
Already!

HORNER
Already, I say; last night I was drunk with half a dozen of your civil persons, as you call'em, and people of Honour, and so was made free of their Society, and dressing rooms for ever hereafter; and am already come to the privileges of sleeping upon their Pallats, warming Smocks, tying Shooes and Garters, and the like Doctor, already, already Doctor.

QUACK
You have made use of your time, Sir.

HORNER
I tell thee, I am now no more interruption to'em, when they sing, or talk bawdy, than a little squab French Page, who speaks no English.

QUACK
But do civil persons, and women of Honour drink, and sing bawdy Songs?

HORNER

O amongst Friends, amongst Friends; for your Bigots in Honour, are just like those in Religion; they fear the eye of the world, more than the eye of Heaven, and think there is no virtue, but railing at vice; and no sin, but giving scandal: They rail at a poor, little, kept Player, and keep themselves some young, modest Pulpit Comedian to be privy to their sins in their Closets, not to tell 'em of them in their Chappels.

QUACK
Nay, the truth on't is, Priests amongst the women now, have quite got the better of us Lay Confessors, Physicians.

HORNER
And they are rather their Patients, but—

[Enter my **LADY FIDGET**, looking about her.

Now we talk of women of Honour, here comes one, step behind the Screen there, and but observe; if I have not particular privileges, with the women of reputation already, Doctor, already.

LADY FIDGET
Well Horner, am not I a woman of Honour? you see I'm as good as my word.

HORNER
And you shall see Madam, I'll not be behind hand with you in honour; and I'll be as good as my word too, if you please but to withdraw into the next room.

LADY FIDGET
But first, my dear Sir, you must promise to have a care of my dear Honour.

HORNER
If you talk a word more of your Honour, you'll make me incapable to wrong it; to talk of Honour in the mysteries of Love, is like talking of Heaven, or the Deity in an operation of Witchcraft, just when you are employing the Devil, it makes the charm impotent.

LADY FIDGET
Nay, fie, let us not be smooty; but you talk of mysteries, and bewitching to me, I don't understand you.

HORNER
I tell you Madam, the word money in a Mistresses mouth, at such a nick of time, is not a more disheartning sound to a younger Brother, than that of Honour to an eager Lover like my self.

LADY FIDGET
But you can't blame a Lady of my reputation to be chary.

HORNER
Chary—I have been chary of it already, by the report I have caus'd of my self.

LADY FIDGET

Ay, but if you shou'd ever let other women know that dear secret, it would come out; nay, you must have a great care of your conduct; for my acquaintance are so censorious, oh 'tis a wicked censorious world, Mr. Horner, I say, are so censorious, and detracting, that perhaps they'll talk to the prejudice of my Honour, though you shou'd not let them know the dear secret.

HORNER
Nay Madam, rather than they shall prejudice your Honour, I'll prejudice theirs; and to serve you, I'll lye with 'em all, make the secret their own, and then they'll keep it: I am a Machiavel in love Madam.

LADY FIDGET
O, no Sir, not that way.

HORNER
Nay, the Devil take me, if censorious women are to be silenc'd any other way.

LADY FIDGET
A secret is better kept I hope, by a single person, than a multitude; therefore pray do not trust any body else with it, dear, dear Mr. Horner.

[Embracing him.

[Enter **SIR JASPAR FIDGET**.

SIR JASPAR
How now!

LADY FIDGET
O my Husband—prevented—and what's almost as bad, found with my arms about another man— that will appear too much—what shall I say? [Aside]. Sir Jaspar come hither, I am trying if Mr. Horner were ticklish, and he's as ticklish as can be, I love to torment the confounded Toad; let you and I tickle him.

SIR JASPAR
No, your Ladyship will tickle him better without me, I suppose, but is this your buying China, I thought you had been at the China House?

HORNER
China-House, that's my Cue, I must take it [Aside]. A Pox, can't you keep your impertinent Wives at home? some men are troubled with the Husbands, but I with the Wives; but I'd have you to know, since I cannot be your Journey-man by night, I will not be your drudge by day, to squire your wife about, and be your man of straw, or scare-crow only to Pyes and Jays; that would be nibling at your forbidden fruit; I shall be shortly the Hackney Gentleman-Usher of the Town.

SIR JASPAR
Heh, heh, he, poor fellow he's in the right on't faith, to squire women about for other folks, is as ungrateful an employment, as to tell money for other folks; [Aside].—heh, he, he, ben't angry Horner—

LADY FIDGET

No, 'tis I have more reason to be angry, who am left by you, to go abroad indecently alone; or, what is more indecent, to pin my self upon such ill bred people of your acquaintance, as this is.

SIR JASPAR
Nay, pr'ythee what has he done?

LADY FIDGET
Nay, he has done nothing.

SIR JASPAR
But what d'ye take ill, if he has done nothing?

LADY FIDGET
Hah, hah, hah, Faith, I can't but laugh however; why d'ye think the unmannerly toad wou'd not come down to me to the Coach, I was fain to come up to fetch him, or go without him, which I 'was resolved not to do; for he knows China very well, and has himself very good, but will not let me see it, lest I should beg some; but I will find it out, and have what I came for yet.

[Exit **LADY FIDGET**, and locks the door, followed by Horner to the door.

HORNER
Lock the door Madam—[Apart to **LADY FIDGET**]. So, she has got into my chamber, and lock'd me out; oh the impertinency of woman-kind! Well Sir Jaspar, plain dealing is a Jewel; if ever you suffer your Wife to trouble me again here, she shall carry you home a pair of Horns, by my Lord Major she shall; though I cannot furnish you my self, you are sure, yet I'll find a way.

SIR JASPAR
Hah, ha, he, at my first coming in, and finding her arms about him, tickling him it seems, I was half jealous, but now I see my folly. [Aside]. Heh, he, he, poor Horner.

HORNER
Nay, though you laugh now, 'twill be my turn e're long: Oh women, more impertinent, more cunning, and more mischievous than their Monkeys, and to me almost as ugly—now is she throwing my things about, and rifling all I have, but I'll get into her the back way, and so rifle her for it—

SIR JASPAR
Hah, ha, ha, poor angry Horner.

HORNER
Stay here a little, I'll ferret her out to you presently, I warrant.

[Exit **HORNER** at t'other door.

SIR JASPAR
Wife, my Lady Fidget, Wife, he is coming into you the back way.

[**SIR JASPAR** calls through the door to his **WIFE**, she answers from within.

LADY FIDGET
Let him come, and welcome, which way he will.

SIR JASPAR
He'll catch you, and use you roughly, and be too strong for you.

LADY FIDGET
Don't you trouble your self, let him if he can.

QUACK [Behind]
This indeed, I cou'd not have believ'd from him, nor any but my own eyes.

[Enter **MISTRISS SQUEAMISH**.

MISTRISS SQUEAMISH
Where's this Woman-hater, this Toad, this ugly, greasie, dirty Sloven?

SIR JASPAR
So the women all will have him ugly, methinks he is a comely person; but his wants make his form contemptible to'em; and 'tis e'en as my Wife said yesterday, talking of him, that a proper handsome Eunuch, was as ridiculous a thing, as a Gigantick Coward.

MISTRISS SQUEAMISH
Sir Jaspar, your Servant, where is the odious Beast?

SIR JASPAR
He's within in his chamber, with my Wife; she's playing the wag with him.

MISTRISS SQUEAMISH
Is she so, and he's a clownish beast, he'll give her no quarter, he'll play the wag with her again, let me tell you; come, let's go help her—What, the door's lock't?

SIR JASPAR
Ay, my Wife lock't it—

MISTRISS SQUEAMISH
Did she so, let us break it open then?

SIR JASPAR
No, no, he'll do her no hurt.

MISTRISS SQUEAMISH
No—But is there no other way to get into 'em, whither goes this? I will disturb'em. [Aside].

[Exit **MISTRISS SQUEAMISH** at another door.

[Enter **OLD LADY SQUEAMISH**.

OLD LADY SQUEAMISH
Where is this Harlotry, this Impudent Baggage, this rambling Tomrigg? O Sir Jaspar, I'm glad to see you here, did you not see my vil'd Grandchild come in hither just now?

SIR JASPAR
Yes,

OLD LADY SQUEAMISH
Ay, but where is she then? where is she? Lord Sir Jaspar I have e'ne ratled my self to pieces in pursuit of her, but can you tell what she makes here, they say below, no woman lodges here.

SIR JASPAR
No.

OLD LADY SQUEAMISH
No—What does she here then? say if it be not a womans lodging, what makes she here? but are you sure no woman lodges here?

SIR JASPAR
No, nor no man neither, this is Mr. Horners Lodging.

OLD LADY SQUEAMISH
Is it so are you sure?

SIR JASPAR
Yes, yes.

OLD LADY SQUEAMISH
So then there's no hurt in't I hope, but where is he?

SIR JASPAR
He's in the next room with my Wife.

OLD LADY SQUEAMISH
Nay if you trust him with your wife, I may with my Biddy, they say he's a merry harmless man now, e'ne as harmless a man as ever came out of Italy with a good voice, and as pretty harmless company for a Lady, as a Snake without his teeth.

SIR JASPAR
Ay. ay poor man.

[Enter **MISTRISS SQUEAMISH**.

MISTRISS SQUEAMISH
I can't find'em—Oh are you here, Grandmother, I follow'd you must know my Lady Fidget hither, 'tis the prettyest lodging, and I have been staring on the prettyest Pictures.

[Enter **LADY FIDGET** with a piece of China in her hand, and **HORNER** following.

LADY FIDGET
And I have been toyling and moyling, for the pretti'st piece of China, my Dear.

HORNER
Nay she has been too hard for me do what I cou'd.

MISTRISS SQUEAMISH
Oh Lord I'le have some China too, good Mr. Horner, don't think to give other people China, and me none, come in with me too.

HORNER
Upon my honour I have none left now.

MISTRISS SQUEAMISH
Nay, nay I have known you deny your China before now, but you shan't put me off so, come—

HORNER
This Lady had the last there.

LADY FIDGET
Yes indeed Madam, to my certain knowledge he has no more left.

MISTRISS SQUEAMISH
O but it may be he may have some you could not find.

LADY FIDGET
What d'y think if he had had any left, I would not have had it too, for we women of quality never think we have China enough.

HORNER
Do not take it ill, I cannot make China for you all, but I will have a Rol-waggon for you too, another time.

MISTRISS SQUEAMISH
Thank you dear Toad. [To **HORNER**, aside.

LADY FIDGET
What do you mean by that promise?

HORNER
Alas she has an innocent, literal understanding. [Apart to **LADY FIDGET**.

OLD LADY SQUEAMISH
Poor Mr. Horner, he has enough to doe to please you all, I see.

HORNER
Ay Madam, you see how they use me.

OLD LADY SQUEAMISH
Poor Gentleman I pitty you.

HORNER
I thank you Madam, I could never find pitty, but from such reverend Ladies as you are, the young ones will never spare a man.

MISTRISS SQUEAMISH
Come come, Beast, and go dine with us, for we shall want a man at Hombre after dinner.

HORNER
That's all their use of me Madam you see.

MISTRISS SQUEAMISH
Come Sloven, I'le lead you to be sure of you.

[Pulls him by the Crevat.

OLD LADY SQUEAMISH
Alas poor man how she tuggs him, kiss, kiss her, that's the way to make such nice women quiet.

HORNER
No Madam, that Remedy is worse than the Torment, they know I dare suffer any thing rather than do it.

OLD LADY SQUEAMISH
Prythee kiss her, and I'le give you her Picture in little, that you admir'd so last night, prythee do.

HORNER
Well nothing but that could bribe me, I love a woman only in Effigie, and good Painting as much as I hate them—I'le do't, for I cou'd adore the Devil well painted.

[Kisses **MISTRISS SQUEAMISH**

MISTRISS SQUEAMISH
Foh, you filthy Toad, nay now I've done jesting.

OLD LADY SQUEAMISH
Ha, ha, ha, I told you so.

MISTRISS SQUEAMISH
Foh a kiss of his—

SIR JASPAR
Has no more hurt in't, than one of my Spaniels.

MISTRISS SQUEAMISH
Nor no more good neither.

QUACK
I will now believe any thing he tells me. [Behind.

[Enter **MR PINCHWIFE**

LADY FIDGET
O Lord here's a man, Sir Jaspar, my Mask, my Mask, I would not be seen here for the world.

SIR JASPAR
What not when I am with you.

LADY FIDGET
No, no my honour—let's be gone.

MISTRISS SQUEAMISH
Oh Grandmother, let us be gone, make hast, make hast, I know not how he may censure us.

LADY FIDGET
Be found in the lodging of any thing like a man, away.

[Exeunt **SIR JASPAR, LADY FIDGET, OLD LADY SQUEAMISH, MISTRISS SQUEAMISH.**

QUACK
What's here another Cuckold—he looks like one, and none else sure have any business with him,
[Behind.

HORNER
Well what brings my dear friend hither?

MR PINCHWIFE
Your impertinency.

HORNER
My impertinency—why you Gentlemen that have got handsome Wives, think you have a privilege of saying any thing to your friends, and are as brutish, as if you were our Creditors.

MR PINCHWIFE
No Sir, I'le ne're trust you any way.

HORNER
But why not, dear Jack, why diffide in me, thou knowst so well.

MR PINCHWIFE
Because I do know you so well.

HORNER
Han't I been always thy friend honest Jack, always ready to serve thee, in love, or battle, before thou wert married, and am so still.

MR PINCHWIFE

I believe so you wou'd be my second now indeed.

HORNER

Well then dear Jack, why so unkind, so grum, so strange to me, come prythee kiss me deare Rogue, gad I was always I say, and am still as much thy Servant as—

MR PINCHWIFE

As I am yours Sir. What you wou'd send a kiss to my Wife, is that it?

HORNER

So there 'tis—a man can't shew his friendship to a married man, but presently he talks of his wife to you, prythee let thy Wife alone, and let thee and I be all one, as we were wont, what thou art as shye of my kindness, as a Lumbard-street Alderman of a Courtiers civility at Lockets.

MR PINCHWIFE

But you are over kind to me, as kind, as if I were your Cuckold already, yet I must confess you ought to be kind and civil to me, since I am so kind, so civil to you, as to bring you this, look you there Sir.

[Delivers him a Letter.

HORNER

What is't?

MR PINCHWIFE

Only a Love Letter Sir.

HORNER

From whom—how, this is from your Wife— hum—and hum—[Reads.

MR PINCHWIFE

Even from my Wife Sir, am I not wondrous kind and civil to you, now too? [Aside]. But you'l not think her so.

HORNER

Ha, is this a trick of his or hers

[Aside.

MR PINCHWIFE

The Gentleman's surpriz'd I find, what you expected a kinder Letter?

HORNER

No faith not I, how cou'd I.

MR PINCHWIFE

Yes yes, I'm sure you did, a man so well made as you are must needs be disappointed, if the women declare not their passion at first sight or opportunity.

HORNER
But what should this mean? stay the Postcript. Be sure you love me whatsoever my husband says to the contrary, and let him not see this, lest he should come home, and pinch me, or kill my Squirrel.
[Reads aside.
It seems he knows not what the Letter contains.

[Aside.

MR PINCHWIFE
Come ne're wonder at it so much.

HORNER
Faith I can't help it.

MR PINCHWIFE
Now I think I have deserv'd your infinite friendship, and kindness, and have shewed my self sufficiently an obliging kind friend and husband, am I not so, to bring a Letter from my Wife to her Gallant?

HORNER
Ay, the Devil take me, art thou, the most obliging, kind friend and husband in the world, ha, ha.

MR PINCHWIFE
Well you may be merry Sir, but in short I must tell you Sir, my honour will suffer no jesting.

HORNER
What do'st thou mean?

MR PINCHWIFE
Does the Letter want a Comment? then know Sir, though I have been so civil a husband, as to bring you a Letter from my Wife, to let you kiss and court her to my face, I will not be a Cuckold Sir, I will not.

HORNER
Thou art mad with jealousie, I never saw thy Wife in my life, but at the Play yesterday, and I know not if it were she or no, I court her, kiss her!

MR PINCHWIFE
I will not be a Cuckold I say, there will be danger in making me a Cuckold.

HORNER
Why, wert thou not well cur'd of thy last clap?

MR PINCHWIFE
I weare a Sword.

HORNER

It should be taken from thee, lest thou should'st do thy self a mischiefe with it, thou art mad, Man.

MR PINCHWIFE
As mad as I am, and as merry as you are, I must have more reason from you e're we part, I say again though you kiss'd, and courted last night my Wife in man's clothes, as she confesses in her Letter.

HORNER
Ha—[Aside.

MR PINCHWIFE
Both she and I say you must not design it again, for you have mistaken your woman, as you have done your man.

HORNER
Oh—I understand something now—[Aside]. Was that thy Wife? why would'st thou not tell me 'twas she? faith my freedome with her was your fault, not mine.

MR PINCHWIFE
Faith so 'twas—[Aside.

HORNER
Fye, I'de never do't to a woman before her husbands face, sure.

MR PINCHWIFE
But I had rather you should do't to my wife before my face, than behind my back, and that you shall never doe.

HORNER
No—you will hinder me.

MR PINCHWIFE
If I would not hinder you, you see by her Letter, she wou'd.

HORNER
Well, I must e'ne acquiess then, and be contented with what she writes.

MR PINCHWIFE
I'le assure you 'twas voluntarily writ, I had no hand in't you may believe me.

HORNER
I do believe thee, faith.

MR PINCHWIFE
And believe her too, for she's an innocent creature, has no dissembling in her, and so fare you well Sir.

HORNER

Pray however present my humble service to her, and tell her I will obey her Letter to a tittle, and fulfill her desires be what they will, or with what difficulty soever I do't, and you shall be no more jealous of me, I warrant her, and you—

MR PINCHWIFE
Well then fare you well, and play with any mans honour but mine, kiss any mans wife but mine, and welcome—

[Exit **MR PINCHWIFE**

HORNER
Ha, ha, ha, Doctor.

QUACK
It seems he has not heard the report of you, or does not believe it.

HORNER
Ha, ha, now Doctor what think you?

QUACK
Pray let's see the Letter—hum—for— deare—love you—

[Reads the Letter.

HORNER
I wonder how she cou'd contrive it! what say'st thou to't, 'tis an Original.

QUACK
So are your Cuckolds too Originals: for they are like no other common Cuckolds, and I will henceforth believe it not impossible for you to Cuckold the Grand Signior amidst his Guards of Eunuchs, that I say—

HORNER
And I say for the Letter, 'tis the first love Letter that ever was without Flames, Darts, Fates, Destinies, Lying and Dissembling in't.

[Enter **SPARKISH** pulling in **MR PINCHWIFE**.

SPARKISH
Come back, you are a pretty Brother-in-law, neither go to Church, nor to dinner with your Sister Bride.

MR PINCHWIFE
My Sister denies her marriage, and you see is gone away from you dissatisfy'd.

SPARKISH
Pshaw, upon a foolish scruple, that our Parson was not in lawful Orders, and did not say all the Common Prayer, but 'tis her modesty only I believe, but let women be never so modest the first day, they'l be sure to come to themselves by night, and I shall have enough of her then; in the mean time, Harry Horner, you must dine with me, I keep my wedding at my Aunts in the Piazza.

HORNER

Thy wedding, what stale Maid has liv'd to despaire of a husband, or what young one of a Gallant?

SPARKISH

O your Servant Sir—this Gentlemans Sister then —No stale Maid.

HORNER

I'm sorry for't.

MR PINCHWIFE

How comes he so concern'd for her—[Aside.

SPARKISH

You sorry for't, why do you know any ill by her?

HORNER

No, I know none but by thee, 'tis for her sake, not yours, and another mans sake that might have hop'd, I thought—

SPARKISH

Another Man, another man, what is his Name?

HORNER

Nay since 'tis past he shall be nameless.
Poor Harcourt I am sorry thou mist her—[Aside

MR PINCHWIFE

He seems to be much troubled at the match—.[Aside.

SPARKISH

Prythee tell me—nay you shan't go Brother.

MR PINCHWIFE

I must of necessity, but I'le come to you to dinner.

[Exit **MR PINCHWIFE.**

SPARKISH

But Harry, what have I a Rival in my Wife already? but withal my heart, for he may be of use to me hereafter, for though my hunger is now my sawce, and I can fall on heartily without, but the time will come, when a Rival will be as good sawce for a married man to a wife, as an Orange to Veale.

HORNER

O thou damn'd Rogue, thou hast set my teeth on edge with thy Orange.

SPARKISH

Then let's to dinner, there I was with you againe, come.

HORNER
But who dines with thee?

SPARKISH
My Friends and Relations, my Brother Pinchwife you see of your acquaintance.

HORNER
And his Wife.

SPARKISH
No gad, he'l nere let her come amongst us good fellows, your stingy country Coxcomb keeps his wife from his friends, as he does his little Firkin of Ale, for his own drinking, and a Gentleman can't get a smack on't, but his servants, when his back is turn'd broach it at their pleasures, and dust it away, ha, ha, ha, gad I am witty, I think, considering I was married to day, by the world, but come—

HORNER
No, I will not dine with you, unless you can fetch her too.

SPARKISH
Pshaw what pleasure can'st thou have with women now, Harry?

HORNER
My eyes are not gone, I love a good prospect yet, and will not dine with you, unless she does too, go fetch her therefore, but do not tell her husband, 'tis for my sake.

SPARKISH
Well I'le go try what I can do, in the mean time come away to my Aunts lodging, 'tis in the way to Pinchwifes.

HORNER
The poor woman has call'd for aid, and stretch'd forth her hand Doctor, I cannot but help her over the Pale out of the Bryars.

[Exeunt **SPARKISH, HORNER, QUACK**

THE SCENE CHANGES TO PINCHWIFE'S HOUSE

MRS PINCHWIFE alone leaning on her elbow.

A Table, Pen, Ink, and Paper.

MRS PINCHWIFE
Well 'tis 'ene so, I have got the London disease, they call Love, I am sick of my Husband, and for my Gallant; I have heard this distemper, call'd a Feaver, but methinks 'tis liker an Ague, for when I think of my Husband, I tremble and am in a cold sweat, and have inclinations to vomit, but when I think of my

Gallant, dear Mr. Horner, my hot fit comes, and I am all in a Feaver, indeed, & as in other Feavers, my own Chamber is tedious to me, and I would fain be remov'd to his, and then methinks I shou'd be well; ah poor Mr. Horner, well I cannot, will not stay here, therefore I'le make an end of my Letter to him, which shall be a finer Letter than my last, because I have studied it like any thing; O Sick, Sick!

[Takes the Pen and writes.

[Enter **MR PINCHWIFE** who seeing her writing steales softly behind her, and looking over her shoulder, snatches the paper from her.

MR PINCHWIFE
What writing more Letters?

MRS PINCHWIFE
O Lord Budd, why d'ye fright me so?

[She offers to run out: he stops her, and reads.

MR PINCHWIFE
How's this! nay you shall not stir Madam.

Deare, Deare, deare, Mr Horner—very well— I have taught you to write Letters to good purpose—but let's see't. First I am to beg your pardon for my boldness in writing to you, which I'de have you to know, I would not have done, had not you said first you lov'd me so extreamly, which if you doe, you will never suffer me to lye in the arms of another man, whom I loath. nauseate, and detest—Now you can write these filthy words but what follows— Therefore I hope you will speedily find some way to free me from this unfortunate match, which was never, I assure you, of my choice, but I'm afraid 'tis already too far gone; however if you love me, as I do you, you will try what you can do, but you must help me away before to morrow, or else alass I shall be for ever out of your reach, for I can defer no longer our—our—what is to follow our— speak what? our Journey into—

[The Letter concludes.

—the Country I suppose—Oh Woman, damn'd Woman, and Love, damn'd Love, their old Tempter, for this is one of his miracles, in a moment, he can make those blind that cou'd see, and those see that were blind, those dumb that could speak, and those prattle who were dumb before, nay what is more than all, make these dow-bak'd, sensless, indocile animals, Women, too hard for us their Politick Lords and Rulers in a moment; But make an end of your Letter, and then I'le make an end of you thus, and all my plagues together.

[Draws his Sword.

MRS PINCHWIFE
O Lord, O Lord you are such a Passionate Man, Budd.

[Enter **SPARKISH**.

SPARKISH

How now what's here to doe.

MR PINCHWIFE
This Fool here now!

SPARKISH
What drawn upon your Wife? you shou'd never do that but at night in the dark when you can't hurt her, this is my Sister in Law is it not? ay faith e'ne our—

[Pulls aside her Handkercheife.

—Country Margery, one may know her, come she and you must go dine with me, dinner's ready, come, but where's my Wife, is she not come home yet, where is she?

MR PINCHWIFE
Making you a Cuckold, 'tis that they all doe, as soon as they can.

SPARKISH
What the Wedding day? no, a Wife that designs to make a Cully of her Husband, will be sure to let him win the first stake of love, by the world, but come they stay dinner for us, come I'le lead down our Margery.

MRS PINCHWIFE
No—Sir go we'l follow you.

SPARKISH
I will not wag without you.

MR PINCHWIFE
This Coxcomb is a sensible torment to me amidst the greatest in the world.

SPARKISH
Come, come Madam Margery.

MR PINCHWIFE
No I'le lead her my way, what wou'd you treat your friends [900] with mine, for want of your own Wife?

[Leads her to t'other door, and locks her in and returns.

I am contented my rage shou'd take breath—[Aside.

SPARKISH
I told Horner this.

MR PINCHWIFE
Come now.

SPARKISH

Lord, how shye you are of your Wife, but let me tell you Brother, we men of wit have amongst us a saying, that Cuckolding like the small Pox comes with a fear, and you may keep your Wife as much as you will out of danger of infection, but if her constitution incline her to't, she'l have it sooner or later by the world, say they.

MR PINCHWIFE

What a thing is a Cuckold, that every fool can make him ridiculous—[Aside]. Well Sir—But let me advise you, now you are come to be concern'd, because you suspect the danger, not to neglect the means to prevent it, especially when the greatest share of the Malady will light upon your own head, for—

How'sere the kind Wife's Belly comes to swell.
The Husband breeds for her, and first is ill.

ACT V

SCENE I

MR. PINCHWIFE'S HOUSE

Enter **MR PINCHWIFE** and **MRS PINCHWIFE**, a Table and Candle.

MR PINCHWIFE

Come take the Pen and make an end of the Letter, just as you intended, if you are false in a tittle, I shall soon perceive it, and punish you with this as you deserve, write what was to follow—let's see—

[Lays his hand on his Sword.

You must make haste and help me away before to morrow, or else I shall be for ever out of your reach, for I can defer no longer our—What follows our?—

MRS PINCHWIFE

Must all out then Budd?— Look you there then.

MRS PINCHWIFE takes the Pen and writes.

MR PINCHWIFE

Let's see—For I can defer no longer our—Wedding—Your slighted Alithea] What's the meaning of this, my Sisters name to't, speak, unriddle?

MRS PINCHWIFE

Yes indeed Budd.

MR PINCHWIFE

But why her name to't speak—speak I say?

MRS PINCHWIFE

Ay but you'l tell her then again, if you wou'd not tell her again.

MR PINCHWIFE
I will not, I am stunn'd, my head turns round, speak.

MRS PINCHWIFE
Won't you tell her indeed, and indeed.

MR PINCHWIFE
No, speak I say.

MRS PINCHWIFE
She'l be angry with me, but I had rather she should be angry with me than you Budd; and to tell you the truth, 'twas she made me write the Letter, and taught me what I should write.

MR PINCHWIFE
Ha—I thought the stile was somewhat better than her own, but how cou'd she come to you to teach you, since I had lock'd you up alone.

MRS PINCHWIFE
O through the key hole Budd.

MR PINCHWIFE
But why should she make you write a Letter for her to him, since she can write her self?

MRS PINCHWIFE
Why she said because—for I was unwilling to do it.

MR PINCHWIFE
Because what—because.

MRS PINCHWIFE
Because lest Mr. Horner should be cruel, and refuse her, or vaine afterwards, and shew the Letter, she might disown it, the hand not being hers.

MR PINCHWIFE
How's this? ha—then I think I shall come to my self again—This changeling cou'd not invent this lye, but if she cou'd, why should she? she might think I should soon discover it—stay—now I think on't too, Horner said he was sorry she had married Sparkish, and her disowning her marriage to me, makes me think she has evaded it, for Horner's sake, yet why should she take this course, but men in love are fools, women may well be so.—[Aside]. But hark you Madam, your Sister went out in the morning, and I have not seen her within since.

MRS PINCHWIFE
A lack a day she has been crying all day above it seems in a corner.

MR PINCHWIFE
Where is she, let me speak with her.

MRS PINCHWIFE

O Lord then he'l discover all—[Aside]. Pray hold Budd, what d'y mean to discover me, she'l know I have told you then, pray Budd let me talk with her first—

MR PINCHWIFE

I must speak with her to know whether Horner ever made her any promise; and whether she be married to Sparkish or no.

MRS PINCHWIFE

Pray dear Budd don't, till I have spoken with her and told her that I have told you all, for she'll kill me else.

MR PINCHWIFE

Go then and bid her come out to me.

MRS PINCHWIFE

Yes, yes Budd—

MR PINCHWIFE

Let me see—

MRS PINCHWIFE

I'le go, but she is not within to come to him, I have just got time to know of Lucy her Maid, who first set me on work, what lye I shall tell next, for I am e'ne at my wits end—

[Exit **MRS PINCHWIFE**.

MR PINCHWIFE

Well I resolve it, Horner shall have her, I'd rather give him my Sister than lend him my Wife, and such an alliance will prevent his pretensions to my Wife sure,—I'le make him of kinn to her, and then he won't care for her,

[**MRS PINCHWIFE** returns.

MRS PINCHWIFE

O Lord Budd I told you what anger you would make me with my Sister.

MR PINCHWIFE

Won't she come hither?

MRS PINCHWIFE

No no, alack a day, she's asham'd to look you in the face, and she says if you go in to her, she'l run away down stairs, and shamefully go her self to Mr. Horner, who has promis'd her marriage she says, and she will have no other, so she won't—

MR PINCHWIFE

Did he so—promise her marriage—then she shall have no other, go tell her so, and if she will come and discourse with me a little concerning the means, I will about it immediately, go—

[Exit **MRS PINCHWIFE**

His estate is equal to Sparkish's, and his extraction as much better than his, as his parts are, but my chief reason is, I'd rather be of kin to him by the name of Brother-in-law, than that of Cuckold— Well what says she now?

[Enter **MRS PINCHWIFE**

MRS PINCHWIFE
Why she says she would only have you lead her to Horners lodging—with whom she first will discourse the matter before she talk with you, which yet she cannot doe; for alack poor creature, she says she can't so much as look you in the face, therefore she'l come to you in a mask, and you must excuse her if she make you no answer to any question of yours, till you have brought her to Mr. Horner, and if you will not chide her, nor question her, she'l come out to you immediately.

MR PINCHWIFE
Let her come I will not speak a word to her, nor require a word from her.

MRS PINCHWIFE
Oh I forgot, besides she says, she cannot look you in the face, though through a mask, therefore wou'd desire you to put out the Candle.

MR PINCHWIFE
I agree to all, let her make haste—there 'tis out—My case—

[Exit **MRS PINCHWIFE** puts out the Candle.

—is something better, I'd rather fight with Horner for not lying with my Sister, than for lying with my Wife, and of the two I had rather find my Sister too forward than my Wife; I expected no other from her free education, as she calls it, and her passion for the Town—well—Wife and Sister are names which make us expect Love and duty, pleasure and comfort, but we find'em plagues and torments, and are equally, though differently troublesome to their keeper; for we have as much a doe to get people to lye with our Sisters, as to keep'em from lying with our Wives.

[Enter **MRS PINCHWIFE** Masked, and in Hoods and Scarves, and a night Gown and Petticoat of Alitheas in the dark.

What are you come Sister? let us go then—but first let me lock up my Wife, Mrs. Margery where are you?

MRS PINCHWIFE
Here Budd.

MR PINCHWIFE
Come hither, that I may lock you up, get you in, Come Sister where are you now?

[Locks the door.

[**MRS PINCHWIFE** gives him her hand, but when he lets her go, she steals softly on t'other side of him, and is lead away by him for his Sister Alithea.

THE SCENE CHANGES TO HORNER'S LODGING.

QUACK. HORNER.

QUACK
What all alone, not so much as one of your Cuckolds here, nor one of their Wives! they use to take their turns with you, as if they were to watch you.

HORNER
Yes it often happens, that a Cuckold is but his Wifes spye, and is more upon family duty, when he is with her gallant abroad hindring his pleasure, than when he is at home with her playing the Gallant, but the hardest duty a married woman imposes upon a lover is, keeping her husband company always.

QUACK
And his fondness wearies you almost as soon as hers.

HORNER
A Pox, keeping a Cuckold company after you have had his Wife, is as tiresome as the company of a Country Squire to a witty fellow of the Town, when he has got all his Mony,

QUACK
And as at first a man makes a friend of the Husband to get the Wife, so at last you are faine to fall out with the Wife to be rid of the Husband.

HORNER
Ay, most Cuckold-makers are true Courtiers, when once a poor man has crack'd his credit for'em, they can't abide to come neer him.

QUACK
But at first to draw him in are so sweet, so kind, so dear, just as you are to Pinchwife, but what becomes of that intrigue with his Wife?

HORNER
A Pox he's as surly as an Alderman that has been bit, and since he's so coy, his Wife's kindness is in vain, for she's a silly innocent.

QUACK
Did she not send you a Letter by him?

HORNER

Yes, but that's a riddle I have not yet solv'd—allow the poor creature to be willing, she is silly too, and he keeps her up so close—

QUACK
Yes, so close that he makes her but the more willing, and adds but revenge to her love, which two when met seldome faile of satisfying each other one way or other.

HORNER
What here's the man we are talking of I think.

[Enter **MR PINCHWIFE** leading in his **WIFE** Masqued, Muffled, and in her Sisters Gown.

HORNER
Pshaw.

QUACK
Bringing his Wife to you is the next thing to bringing a Love Letter from her.

HORNER
What means this?

MR PINCHWIFE
The last time you know Sir I brought you a love Letter, now you see a Mistress, I think you'l say I am a civil man to you.

HORNER
Ay the Devil take me will I say thou art the civillest man I ever met with, and I have known some; I fancy, I understand thee now, better than I did the Letter, but hark thee in thy eare—

MR PINCHWIFE
What?

HORNER
Nothing but the usual question man, is she found on thy word?

MR PINCHWIFE
What you take her for a wench and me for a Pimp?

HORNER
Pshaw, wench and Pimp, paw words, I know thou art an honest fellow, and hast a great acquaintance among the Ladies, and perhaps hast made love for me rather than let me make love to thy Wise—

MR PINCHWIFE
Come Sir, in short, I am for no fooling.

HORNER
Nor I neither, therefore prythee let's see her face presently, make her show man, art thou sure I don't know her?

MR PINCHWIFE
I am sure you doe know her.

HORNER
A Pox why dost thou bring her to me then?

MR PINCHWIFE
Because she's a Relation of mine.

HORNER
Is she faith man, then thou art still more civil and obliging, dear Rogue.

MR PINCHWIFE
Who desir'd me to bring her to you.

HORNER
Then she is obliging, dear Rogue.

MR PINCHWIFE
You'l make her welcome for my sake I hope.

HORNER
I hope she is handsome enough to make her self wellcome; prythee let her unmask.

MR PINCHWIFE
Doe you speak to her, she wou'd never be rul'd by me.

HORNER
Madam—

[**MRS PINCHWIFE** whispers to **HORNER**

She says she must speak with me in private, withdraw prythee.

MR PINCHWIFE
She's unwilling it seems I shou'd know all her undecent conduct in this business—[Aside]. Wel then Ile leave you together, and hope when I am gone you'l agree, if not you and I shan't agree Sir.—

HORNER
What means the Fool?—if she and I agree 'tis no matter what you and I do.

[Whispers to **MRS PINCHWIFE**, who makes signs with her hand for him to be gone.]

MR PINCHWIFE
In the mean time I'le fetch a Parson, and find out Sporkish and disabuse him. You wou'd have me fetch a Parson, would you not, well then —Now I think I am rid of her, and shall have no more trouble with

her—Our Sisters and Daughters like Usurers money, are safest, when put out; but our Wifes, like their writings, never safe, but in our Closets under Lock and Key.

[Exit **MR PINCHWIFE**

[Enter **BOY**.

BOY
Sir Jaspar Fidget Sir is coming up.

HORNER
Here's the trouble of a Cuckold, now we are talking of, a pox on him, has he not enough to doe to hinder his Wifes sport, but he must other women's too.—Step in here Madam.

[Exit **MRS PINCHWIFE**

[Enter **SIR JASPAR**.

SIR JASPAR
My best and dearest Friend.

HORNER
The old stile Doctor— Well be short, for I am busie, what would your impertinent Wife have now?

SIR JASPAR
Well guess'd y' faith, for I do come from her.

HORNER
To invite me to supper, tell her I can't come, go.

SIR JASPAR
Nay, now you are out faith, for my Lady and the whole knot of the virtuous gang, as they call themselves, are resolv'd upon a frolick of coming to you to night in a Masquerade, and are all drest already.

HORNER
I shan't be at home.

SIR JASPAR
Lord how churlish he is to women—nay prythee don't disappoint'em, they'l think 'tis my fault, prythee don't, I'le send in the Banquet and the Fiddles, but make no noise on't, for the poor virtuous Rogues would not have it known for the world, that they go a Masquerading, and they would come to no mans Ball, but yours.

HORNER
Well, well—get you gone, and tell'em if they come, 'twill be at the peril of their honour and yours.

SIR JASPAR

Heh, he, he—we'l trust you for that, farewell—

[Exit **SIR JASPAR**.

HORNER
Doctor anon you too shall be my guest.
But now I'm going to a private feast.

THE SCENE CHANGES TO THE PIAZZA OF COVENT GARDEN.

SPARKISH, MR PINCHWIFE.

SPARKISH with the Letter in his hand.

SPARKISH
But who would have thought a woman could have been false to me, by the world, I could not have thought it.

MR PINCHWIFE
You were for giving and taking liberty, she has taken it only Sir, now you find in that Letter, you are a frank person, and so is she you see there.

SPARKISH
Nay if this be her hand—for I never saw it.

MR PINCHWIFE
'Tis no matter whether that be her hand or no, I am sure this hand at her desire lead her to Mr. Horner, with whom I left her just now, to go fetch a Parson to'em at their desire too, to deprive you of her for ever, for it seems yours was but a mock marriage.

SPARKISH
Indeed she wou'd needs have it that 'twas Harcourt himself in a Parsons habit, that married us, but I'm sure he told me 'twas his Brother Ned.

MR PINCHWIFE
O there 'tis out and you were deceiv'd not she, for you are such a frank person—but I must be gone—you'l find her at Mr. Horners, goe and believe your eyes.

[Exit **MR PINCHWIFE**

SPARKISH
Nay I'le to her, and call her as many Crocodiles, Syrens, Harpies, and other heathenish names, as a Poet would do a Mistress, who had refus'd to heare his suit, nay more his Verses on her. But stay, is not that she following a Torch at t'other end of the Piazza, and from Horners certainly—'tis so—

[Enter **ALITHEA** following a Torch, and **LUCY** behind.

You are well met Madam though you don't think so; what you have made a short visit to Mr. Horner, but I suppose you'l return to him presently, by that time the Parson can be with him.

ALITHEA
Mr. Horner, and the Parson Sir—

SPARKISH
Come Madam no more dissembling, no more jilting for I am no more a frank person.

ALITHEA
How's this.

LUCY
So 'twill work I see—[Aside.

SPARKISH
Cou'd you find out no easie Country Fool to abuse? none but me, a Gentleman of wit and pleasure about the Town, but it was your pride to be too hard for a man of parts, unworthy false woman, false as a friend that lends a man mony to lose, false as dice, who undoe those that trust all they have to'em.

LUCY
He has been a great bubble by his similes as they say—[Aside.

ALITHEA
You have been too merry Sir at your wedding dinner sure.

SPARKISH
What d'y mock me too?

ALITHEA
Or you have been deluded.

SPARKISH
By you.

ALITHEA
Let me understand you.

SPARKISH
Have you the confidence, I should call it something else, since you know your guilt, to stand my just reproaches? you did not write an impudent Letter to Mr. Horner, who I find now has club'd with you in deluding me with his aversion for women, that I might not forsooth suspect him for my Rival.

LUCY
D'y think the Gentleman can be jealous now Madam—[Aside.

ALITHEA

I write a Letter to Mr. Horner!

SPARKISH
Nay Madam, do not deny it, your Brother shew'd it me just now, and told me likewise he left you at Horners lodging to fetch a Parson to marry you to him, and I wish you joy Madam, joy, joy, and to him too much joy, and to my self more joy for not marrying you.

ALITHEA
So I find my Brother would break off the match, and I can consent to't, since I see this Gentleman can be made jealous. [Aside]. O Lucy, by his rude usage and jealousie, he makes me almost afraid I am married to him, art thou sure 'twas Harcourt himself and no Parson that married us.

SPARKISH
No Madam I thank you, I suppose that was a contrivance too of Mr. Horners and yours, to make Harcourt play the Parson, but I would as little as you have him one now, no not for the world, for shall I tell you another truth, I never had any passion for you, 'till now, for now I hate you, 'tis true I might have married your portion, as other men of parts of the Town do sometimes, and so your Servant, and to shew my unconcernedness, I'le come to your wedding, and resign you with as much joy as I would a stale wench to a new Cully, nay with as much joy as I would after the first night, if I had been married to you, there's for you, and so your Servant, Servant.

[Exit **SPARKISH**

ALITHEA
How was I deceiv'd in a man!

LUCY
You'l believe then a fool may be made jealous now? for that easiness in him that suffers him to be led by a Wife, will likewise permit him to be perswaded against her by others.

ALITHEA
But marry Mr. Horner, my brother does not intend it sure; if I thought he did, I would take thy advice, and Mr. Harcourt for my Husband, and now I wish, that if there be any over-wise woman of the Town, who like me would marry a fool, for fortune, liberty, or title, first that her husband may love Play, and be a Cully to all the Town, but her, and suffer none but fortune to be mistress of his purse, then if for liberty, that he may send her into the Country under the conduct of some housewifely mother-in law; and if for title, may the world give 'em none but that of Cuckold.

LUCY
And for her greater curse Madam, may he not deserve it.

ALITHEA
Away impertinent—is not this my old Lady Lanterlus?

LUCY
Yes Madam. [Aside]. and here I hope we shall find Mr. Harcourt—

[Exeunt **ALITHEA, LUCY**

HORNER, LADY FIDGET, MRS DAINTY FIDGET, MISTRISS SQUEAMISH, a Table, Banquet, and Bottles.

HORNER
A Pox they are come too soon—before I have sent back my new—Mistress, all I have now to do, is to lock her in, that they may not see her—[Aside.

LADY FIDGET
That we may be sure of our wellcome, we have brought our entertainment with us, and are resolv'd to treat thee, dear Toad.

MRS DAINTY FIDGET
And that we may be merry to purpose, have left Sir Jaspar and my old Lady Squeamish quarrelling at home at Baggammon.

MISTRISS SQUEAMISH
Therefore let us make use of our time, lest they should chance to interrupt us.

LADY FIDGET
Let us sit then.

HORNER
First that you may be private, let me lock this door, and that, and I'le wait upon you presently.

LADY FIDGET
No Sir, shut 'em only and your lips for ever, for we must trust you as much as our women.

HORNER
You know all vanity's kill'd in me, I have no occasion for talking.

LADY FIDGET
Now Ladies, supposing we had drank each of us our two Bottles, let us speak the truth of our hearts.

MRS DAINTY FIDGET and **MISTRISS SQUEAMISH**
Agreed.

LADY FIDGET
By this brimmer, for truth is no where else to be found,
Not in thy heart false man. [Aside to **HORNER**

HORNER
You have found me a true man I'm sure. [Aside to **LADY FIDGET**.

LADY FIDGET

Not every way—[Aside to **HORNER**
But let us sit and be Merry.

LADY FIDGET sings.
I.
Why should our damn'd Tyrants oblige us to live,
On the pittance of Pleasure which they only give.
We must not rejoyce,
With Wine and with noise.
In vaine we must wake in a dull bed alone.
Whilst to our warm Rival the Bottle, they're gone.
Then lay aside charms,
And take up these arms

II.
'Tis Wine only gives 'em their Courage and Wit,
Because we live sober to men we submit.
If for Beauties you'd pass.
Take a lick of the Glass.
'Twill mend your complexions, and when they are gone,
The best red we have is the red of the Grape.
Then Sisters lay't on.
And dam a good shape.

MRS DAINTY FIDGET
Dear Brimmer, well in token of our openness and plain dealing, let us throw our Masques over our heads.

HORNER
So 'twill come to the Glasses anon.

MISTRISS SQUEAMISH
Lovely Brimmer, let me enjoy him first.

LADY FIDGET
No, I never part with a Gallant, till I've try'd him. Dear Brimmer that mak'st our Husbands short sighted.

MRS DAINTY FIDGET
And our bashful gallants bold.

MISTRISS SQUEAMISH
And for want of a Gallant, the Butler lovely in our eyes, drink Eunuch.

LADY FIDGET
Drink thou representative of a Husband, damn a Husband.

MRS DAINTY FIDGET
And as it were a Husband, an old keeper.

MISTRISS SQUEAMISH
And an old Grandmother.

HORNER
And an English Bawd, and a French Chirurgion.

LADY FIDGET
Ay we have all reason to curse 'em.

HORNER
For my sake Ladies.

LADY FIDGET
No, for our own, for the first spoils all young gallants industry.

MRS DAINTY FIDGET
And the others art makes 'em bold only with common women.

MISTRISS SQUEAMISH
And rather run the hazard of the vile distemper amongst them, than of a denial amongst us.

MRS DAINTY FIDGET
The filthy Toads chuse Mistresses now, as they do Stuffs, for having been fancy'd and worn by others.

MISTRISS SQUEAMISH
For being common and cheap.

LADY FIDGET
Whilst women of quality, like the richest Stuffs, lye untumbled, and unask'd for.

HORNER
Ay neat, and cheap, and new often they think best.

MRS DAINTY FIDGET
No Sir, the Beasts will be known by a Mistriss longer than by a suit.

MISTRISS SQUEAMISH
And 'tis not for cheapness neither.

LADY FIDGET
No, for the vain fopps will take up Druggets, and embroider 'em, but I wonder at the depraved appetites of witty men, they use to be out of the common road, and hate imitation, pray tell me beast, when you were a man, why you rather chose to club with a multitude in a common house, for an entertainment, than to be the only guest at a good Table.

HORNER

Why faith ceremony and expectation are unsufferable to those that are sharp bent, people always eat with the best stomach at an ordinary, where every man is snatching for the best bit.

LADY FIDGET
Though he get a cut over the fingers—but I have heard people eat most heartily of another man's meat, that is, what they do not pay for.

HORNER
When they are sure of their wellcome and freedome, for ceremony in love and eating, is as ridiculous as in fighting, falling on briskly is all should be done in those occasions.

LADY FIDGET
Well then let me tell you Sir, there is no where more freedome than in our houses, and we take freedom from a young person as a sign of good breeding, and a person may be as free as he pleases with us, as frolick, as gamesome, as wild as he will.

HORNER
Han't I heard you all declaim against wild men.

LADY FIDGET
Yes, but for all that, we think wildness in a man, as desirable a quality, as in a Duck, or Rabbet; a tame man, foh.

HORNER
I know not, but your Reputations frightned me, as much as your Faces invited me.

LADY FIDGET
Our Reputation, Lord! Why should you not think, that we women make use of our Reputation, as you men of yours, only to deceive the world with less suspicion; our virtue is like the State-man's Religion, the Quakers Word, the Gamesters Oath, and the Great Man's Honour, but to cheat those that trust us.

MISTRISS SQUEAMISH
And that Demureness, Coyness, and Modesty, that you see in our Faces in the Boxes at Plays, is as much a sign of a kind woman, as a Vizard-mask in the Pit.

MRS DAINTY FIDGET
For I assure you, women are least mask'd, when they have the Velvet Vizard on.

LADY FIDGET
You wou'd have found us modest women in our denyals only.

MISTRISS SQUEAMISH
Our bashfulness is only the reflection of the Men's.

MRS DAINTY FIDGET
We blush, when they are shame-fac'd.

HORNER

I beg your pardon Ladies, I was deceiv'd in you devilishly, but why, that mighty pretence to Honour?

LADY FIDGET
We have told you; but sometimes 'twas for the same reason you men pretend business often, to avoid ill company, to enjoy the better, and more privately those you love.

HORNER
But why, wou'd you ne'er give a Friend a wink then?

LADY FIDGET
Faith, your Reputation frightned us as much, as ours did you, you were so notoriously lewd.

HORNER
And you so seemingly honest.

LADY FIDGET
Was that all that deterr'd you?

HORNER
And so expensive—you allow freedom you say.

LADY FIDGET
Ay, ay.

HORNER
That I was afraid of losing my little money, as well as my little time, both which my other pleasures required.

LADY FIDGET
Money, foh—you talk like a little fellow now, do such as we expect money?

HORNER
I beg your pardon, Madam, I must confess, I have heard that great Ladies, like great Merchants, set but the higher prizes upon what they have, because they are not in necessity of taking the first offer.

MRS DAINTY FIDGET
Such as we, make sale of our hearts?

MISTRISS SQUEAMISH
We brib'd for our Love? Foh.

HORNER
With your pardon, Ladies, I know, like great men in Offices, you seem to exact flattery and attendance only from your Followers, but you have receivers about you, and such fees to pay, a man is afraid to pass your Grants; besides we must let you win at Cards, or we lose your hearts; and if you make an assignation, 'tis at a Goldsmiths, Jewellers, or China house, where for your Honour, you deposit to him, he must pawn his, to the punctual Citt, and so paying for what you take up, pays for what he takes up.

MRS DAINTY FIDGET
Wou'd you not have us assur'd of our Gallants Love?

MISTRISS SQUEAMISH
For Love is better known by Liberality, than by Jealousie.

LADY FIDGET
For one may be dissembled, the other not—but my Jealousie can be no longer dissembled, and they are telling ripe: [Aside]. Come here's to our Gallants in waiting, whom we must name, and I'll begin, this is my false Rogue.

[Claps him on the back.

MISTRISS SQUEAMISH
How!

HORNER
So all will out now—

MISTRISS SQUEAMISH
Did you not tell me, 'twas for my sake only, you reported your self no man? [Aside to **HORNER**.

MRS DAINTY FIDGET
Oh Wretch! did you not swear to me, 'twas for my Love, and Honour, you pass'd for that thing you do? [Aside to **HORNER**.

HORNER
So, so.

LADY FIDGET
Come, speak Ladies, this is my false Villain.

MISTRISS SQUEAMISH
And mine too.

MRS DAINTY FIDGET
And mine.

HORNER
Well then, you are all three my false Rogues too, and there's an end on't.

LADY FIDGET
Well then, there's no remedy, Sister Sharers, let us not fall out, but have a care of our Honour; though we get no Presents, no Jewels of him, we are savers of our Honour, the Jewel of most value and use, which shines yet to the world unsuspected, though it be counterfeit.

HORNER

Nay, and is e'en as good, as if it were true, provided the world think so; for Honour, like Beauty now, only depends on the opinion of others.

LADY FIDGET
Well Harry Common, I hope you can be true to three, swear, but 'tis no purpose, to require your Oath; for you are as often forsworn, as you swear to new women.

HORNER
Come, faith Madam, let us e'en pardon one another, for all the difference I find betwixt we men, and you women, we forswear our selves at the beginning of an Amour, you, as long as it lasts.

[Enter **SIR JASPAR FIDGET** and **OLD LADY FIDGET**.

SIR JASPAR
Oh my Lady Fidget, was this your cunning, to come to Mr. Horner without me; but you have been no where else I hope.

LADY FIDGET
No, Sir Jaspar.

OLD LADY SQUEAMISH
And you came straight hither Biddy.

MISTRISS SQUEAMISH
Yes indeed, Lady Grandmother.

SIR JASPAR
'Tis well, 'tis well, I knew when once they were throughly acquainted with poor Horner, they'd ne'er be from him; you may let her masquerade it with my Wife, and Horner, and I warrant her Reputation safe.

[Enter **BOY**.

BOY
O Sir, here's the Gentleman come, whom you bid me not suffer to come up, without giving you notice, with a Lady too, and other Gentlemen—

HORNER
Do you all go in there, whil'st I send 'em away, and Boy, do you desire 'em to stay below 'til I come, which shall be immediately.

[Exeunt **SIR JASPAR, OLD LADY MISTRISS SQUEAMISH, LADY FIDGET, MRS DAINTY FIDGET, MISTRISS SQUEAMISH.**

BOY
Yes Sir.

[Exit.

[Exit **HORNER** at t'other door, and returns with **MRS PINCHWIFE**.

HORNER
You wou'd not take my advice to be gone home, before your Husband came back, he'll now discover all, yet pray my Dearest be perswaded to go home, and leave the rest to my management, I'll let you down the back way.

MRS PINCHWIFE
I don't know the way home, so I don't.

HORNER
My man shall wait upon you.

MRS PINCHWIFE
No, don't you believe, that I'll go at all; what are you weary of me already?

HORNER
No my life, 'tis that I may love you long, 'tis to secure my love, and your Reputation with your Husband, he'll never receive you again else.

MRS PINCHWIFE
What care I, d'ye think to frighten me with that? I don't intend to go to him again; you shall be my Husband now.

HORNER
I cannot be your Husband, Dearest, since you are married to him.

MRS PINCHWIFE
O wou'd you make me believe that—don't I see every day at London here, women leave their first Husband, and go, and live with other men as their Wives, pish, pshaw, you'd make me angry, but that I love you so mainly.

HORNER
So, they are coming up—In again, in, I hear 'em:

[Exit **MRS PINCHWIFE**.

Well, a silly Mistriss, is like a weak place, soon got, soon lost, a man has scarce time for plunder; she betrays her Husband, first to her Gallant, and then her Gallant, to her Husband.

[Enter **MR PINCHWIFE, ALITHEA, HARCOURT, SPARKISH, LUCY**, and a **PARSON**.

MR PINCHWIFE
Come Madam, 'tis not the sudden change of your dress, the confidence of your asseverations, and your false witness there, shall perswade me, I did not bring you hither, just now; here's my witness, who cannot deny it, since you must be confronted—Mr. Horner, did not I bring this Lady to you just now?

HORNER

Now must I wrong one woman for anothers sake, but that's no new thing with me; for in these cases I am still on the criminal's side, against the innocent. [Aside.

ALITHEA
Pray, speak Sir.

HORNER
It must be so—I must be impudent, and try my luck, impudence uses to be too hard for truth. [Aside.

MR PINCHWIFE
What, you are studying an evasion, or excuse for her, speak Sir.

HORNER
No faith, I am something backward only, to speak in womens affairs or disputes.

MR PINCHWIFE
She bids you speak.

ALITHEA
Ay, pray Sir do, pray satisfie him,

HORNER
Then truly, you did bring that Lady to me just now,

MR PINCHWIFE
O ho—

ALITHEA
How Sir—

HARCOURT
How, Horner!

ALITHEA
What mean you Sir, I always took you for a man of Honour?

HORNER
Ay, so much a man of Honour, that I must save my Mistriss, I thank you, come what will on't. [Aside.

SPARKISH
So if I had had her, she'd have made me believe, the Moon had been made of a Christmas pye.

LUCY
Now cou'd I speak, if I durst, and 'solve the Riddle, who am the Author of it. [Aside.

ALITHEA
O unfortunate Woman! a combination against my Honour, which most concerns me now, because you share in my disgrace, Sir, and it is your censure which I must now suffer, that troubles me, not theirs.

HARCOURT

Madam, then have no trouble, you shall now see 'tis possible for me to love too, without being jealous, I will not only believe your innocence my self, but make all the world believe it— Horner I must now be concern'd for this Ladies Honour.

[Apart to **HORNER**.

HORNER

And I must be concern'd for a Ladies Honour too.

HARCOURT

This Lady has her Honour, and I will protect it.

HORNER

My Lady has not her Honour, but has given it me to keep, and I will preserve it.

HARCOURT

I understand you not

HORNER

I wou'd not have you.

MRS PINCHWIFE

What's the matter with 'em all

[**MRS PINCHWIFE** peeping in behind.

MR PINCHWIFE

Come, come, Mr. Horner, no more disputing, here's the Parson, I brought him not in vain.

HORNER

No Sir, I'll employ him, if this Lady please.

MR PINCHWIFE

How, what d'ye mean?

SPARKISH

Ay, what does he mean?

HORNER

Why, I have resign'd your Sister to him, he has my consent.

MR PINCHWIFE

But he has not mine Sir, a womans injur'd Honour, no more than a man's, can be repair'd or satisfied by any, but him that first wrong'd it; and you shall marry her presently, or—

[Lays his hand on his Sword.

[Enter to them **MRS PINCHWIFE**.

MRS PINCHWIFE
O Lord, they'll kill poor Mr. Horner, besides he shan't marry her, whilest I stand by, and look on, I'll not lose my second Husband so.

MR PINCHWIFE
What do I see?

ALITHEA
My Sister in my cloaths!

SPARKISH
Ha!

MRS PINCHWIFE
Nay, pray now don't quarrel about finding work for the Parson, he shall marry me to Mr. Horner; for now I believe, you have enough of me. [To **MR PINCHWIFE**].

HORNER
Damn'd, damn'd loving Changeling.

MRS PINCHWIFE
Pray Sister, pardon me for telling so many lyes of you.

HARCOURT
I suppose the Riddle is plain now.

LUCY
No, that must be my work, good Sir, hear me.

Kneels to **MR PINCHWIFE**, who stands doggedly, with his hat over his eyes.

MR PINCHWIFE
I will never hear woman again, but make 'em all silent, thus—

[Offers to draw upon his **WIFE**.

HORNER
No, that must not be.

MR PINCHWIFE
You then shall go first, 'tis all one to me.

Offers to draw on **HORNER** stopt by **HARCOURT**.

HARCOURT

Hold—

[Enter **SIR JASPAR FIDGET, LADY FIDGET, OLD LADY SQUEAMISH, MRS DAINTY FIDGET, MRS SQUEAMISH**.

SIR JASPAR
What's the matter, what's the matter, pray what's the matter Sir, I beseech you communicate Sir.

MR PINCHWIFE
Why my Wife has communicated Sir, as your Wife may have done too Sir, if she knows him Sir—

SIR JASPAR
Pshaw, with him, ha, ha, he.

MR PINCHWIFE
D'ye mock me Sir, a Cuckold is a kind of a wild Beast, have a care Sir—

SIR JASPAR
No sure, you mock me Sir—he cuckold you! it can't be, ha, ha, he, why, I'll tell you Sir.

[Offers to whisper.

MR PINCHWIFE
I tell you again, he has whor'd my Wife, and yours too, if he knows her, and all the women he comes near; 'tis not his dissembling, his hypocrisie can wheedle me.

SIR JASPAR
How does he dissemble, is he a Hypocrite? nay then—how—Wife—Sister is he an Hypocrite?

OLD LADY SQUEAMISH
An Hypocrite, a dissembler, speak young Harlotry, speak how?

SIR JASPAR
Nay then—O my head too—O thou libinous Lady!

OLD LADYSQUEAMISH
O thou Harloting, Harlotry, hast thou don't then?

SIR JASPAR
Speak good Horner, art thou a dissembler, a Rogue? hast thou—

HORNER
Soh—

LUCY
I'll fetch you off, and her too, if she will but hold her tongue. [Apart to **HORNER**

HORNER

Canst thou? I'll give thee—[Apart to **LUCY**.

LUCY [to **MR PINCHWIFE**]
Pray have but patience to hear me Sir, who am the unfortunate cause of all this confusion, your Wife is innocent, I only culpable; for I put her upon telling you all these lyes, concerning my Mistress, in order to the breaking off the match, between Mr. Sparkish and her, to make way for Mr. Harcourt.

SPARKISH
Did you so eternal Rotten-tooth, then it seems my Mistress was not false to me, I was only deceiv'd by you, brother that shou'd have been, now man of conduct, who is a frank person now, to bring your Wife to her Lover— ha—

LUCY
I assure you Sir, she came not to Mr. Horner out of love, for she loves him no more—

MRS PINCHWIFE
Hold, I told lyes for you, but you shall tell none for me, for I do love Mr. Horner with all my soul, and no body shall say me nay; pray don't you go to make poor Mr. Horner believe to the contrary, 'tis spitefully done of you, I'm sure.

HORNER
Peace, Dear Ideot. [Aside to **MRS PINCHWIFE**

MRS PINCHWIFE
Nay, I will not peace.

MR PINCHWIFE
Not 'til I make you.

[Enter **DORILANT, QUACK**

DORILANT
Horner, your Servant, I am the Doctors Guest, he must excuse our intrusion.

QUACK
But what's the matter Gentlemen, for Heavens sake, what's the matter?

HORNER
Oh 'tis well you are come—'tis a censorious world we live in, you may have brought me a reprieve, or else I had died for a crime, I never committed, and these innocent Ladies had suffer'd with me, therefore pray satisfie these worthy, honourable, jealous Gentlemen [Whispers].—that—

QUACK
O I understand you, is that all—Sir Jasper, by heavens and upon the word of a Physician [Whispers to **SIR JASPAR**]. Sir,—

SIR JASPAR
Nay I do believe you truly—pardon me my virtuous Lady, and dear of honour.

OLD LADY SQUEAMISH
What then all's right again.

SIR JASPAR
Ay, ay, and now let us satisfie him too.

They whisper with **MR PINCHWIFE**

MR PINCHWIFE
An Eunuch! pray no fooling with me.

QUACK
I'le bring half the Chirurgions in Town to swear it.

MR PINCHWIFE
They—they'l sweare a man that bled to death through his wounds died of an Apoplexy.

QUACK
Pray hear me Sir—why all the Town has heard the report of him.

MR PINCHWIFE
But does all the Town believe it.

QUACK
Pray inquire a little, and first of all these.

MR PINCHWIFE
I'm sure when I left the Town he was the lewdest fellow in't.

QUACK
I tell you Sir he has been in France since, pray ask but these Ladies and Gentlemen, your friend Mr. Dorilant, Gentlemen and Ladies, han't you all heard the late sad report of poor Mr. Horner.

ALL LADIES
Ay, ay, ay.

DORILANT
Why thou jealous Fool do'st thou doubt it, he's an errant French Capon.

MRS PINCHWIFE
'Tis false Sir, you shall not disparage poor Mr. Horner, for to my certain knowledge—

LUCY
O hold—

MISTRISS SQUEAMISH
Stop her mouth—[Aside to **LUCY**

MRS DAINTY FIDGET
Upon my honour Sir, 'tis as true. [To **MR PINCHWIFE**.

MRS DAINTY FIDGET
D'y think we would have been seen in his company—

MISTRISS SQUEAMISH
Trust our unspotted reputations with him!

MRS DAINTY FIDGET
This you get, and we too, by trusting your secret to a fool—

[Aside to **HORNER**

HORNER
Peace Madam,—[Aside to **QUACK** well Doctor is not this a good design that carryes a man on unsuspected, and brings him off safe.—

MR PINCHWIFE
Well, if this were true, but my Wife—[Aside

[**DORILANT** whispers with **MRS PINCHWIFE**

ALITHEA
Come Brother your Wife is yet innocent you see, but have a care of too strong an imagination, least like an over-concern'd timerous Gamester by fancying an unlucky cast it should come, Women and Fortune are truest still to those that trust 'em.

LUCY
And any wild thing grows but the more fierce and hungry for being kept up, and more dangerous to the Keeper.

ALITHEA
There's doctrine for all Husbands Mr. Harcourt.

HARCOURT
I edifie Madam so much, that I am impatient till I am one.

DORILANT
And I edifie so much by example I will never be one.

LUCY
And because I will not disparage my parts I'le ne're be one.

HORNER
And I alass can't be one.

MR PINCHWIFE

But I must be one—against my will to a Country-Wife, with a Country-murrain to me.

MRS PINCHWIFE

And I must be a Country Wife still too I find, for I can't like a City one, be rid of my musty Husband and doe what I list.

[Aside.

HORNER

Now Sir I must pronounce your Wife Innocent, though I blush whilst I do it, and I am the only man by her now expos'd to shame, which I will straight drown in Wine, as you shall your suspition, and the Ladies troubles we'l divert with a Ballet, Doctor where are your Maskers.

LUCY

Indeed she's Innocent Sir, I am her witness, and her end of coming out was but to see her Sisters Wedding, and what she has said to your face of her love to Mr. Horner was but the usual innocent revenge on a Husbands jealousie, was it not Madam speak—

MRS PINCHWIFE

Since you'l have me tell more lyes—[Aside to **LUCY** and **HORNER**].
Yes indeed Budd.

MR PINCHWIFE

For my own sake fain I wou'd all believe.
Cuckolds like Lovers shou'd themselves deceive.
But [—sighs—
His honour is least safe, (too late I find)
Who trusts it with a foolish Wife or Friend.
A Dance of Cuckolds.

HORNER

Vain Fopps, but court, and dress, and keep a puther,
To pass for Womens men, with one another.
But he who aimes by women to be priz'd,
First by the men you see must be despis'd.

EPILOGUE spoken by Mr. Hart:

Now you the Vigorous, who dayly here
O're Vizard-Mask, in publick dominere,
And what you'd doe to her if in Place where;
Nay have the confidence, to cry come out,
Yet when she says lead on, you are not stout;
But to your well-drest Brother straight turn round
And cry, Pox on her Ned, she can't be sound:

Then slink away, a fresh one to ingage,
With so much seeming heat and loving Rage,
You'd frighten listning Actress on the Stage:
Till she at last has seen you huffing come,
And talk of keeping in the Tyreing-Room,
Yet cannot be provok'd to lead her home:
Next you Fallstaffs of fifty, who beset
Your Buckram Maidenheads, which your friends get;
And whilst to them, you of Atchievements boast,
They share the booty, and laugh at your cost.
In fine, you Essens't Boyes, both Old and Young,
Who wou'd be thought so eager, brisk, and strong,
Yet do the Ladies, not their Husbands, wrong:
Whose Purses for your manhood make excuse,
And keep your Flanders Mares for shew, not use;
Encourag'd by our Womans Man to day,
A Horners part may vainly think to Play;
And may Intreagues so bashfully disown
That they may doubted be by few or none,
May kiss the Cards at Picquet, Hombre,—Lu,
And so be thought to kiss the Lady too;
But Gallants, have a care faith, what you do.
The World, which to no man his due will give,
You by experience know you can deceive,
And men may still believe you Vigorous,
But then we Women,—there's no cous'ning us.

CPSIA information can be obtained
at www.ICGtesting.com
Printed in the USA
LVHW041954291119
638856LV00011B/729/P